God's World, God's Body

God's World, God's Body

Grace Jantzen

Foreword by
JOHN MACQUARRIE

THE WESTMINSTER PRESS
Philadelphia

Copyright © 1984 Grace M. Jantzen

First published in the United States by
The Westminster Press®
Philadelphia, Pennsylvania

PRINTED IN THE UNITED STATES OF AMERICA
9 8 7 6 5 4 3 2 1

Library of Congress Cataloging in Publication Data

Jantzen, Grace.
  God's world, God's body.

  Bibliography: p.
  Includes index.
  1. God. 2. Theology, Doctrinal. I. Title.
BT102.J35 1984   231   84-3697
ISBN 0-664-24619-2

To My Sister

Sanctus, Sanctus, Sanctus
Dominus Deus Sabaoth
Pleni sunt coeli et terra gloria tua.

Contents

Foreword

That God is a purely spiritual being, immaterial, invisible, intangible, is assumed to be a basic truth by the great majority of those who believe in God. To suggest that God might have a body would seem absurd to virtually all of those believers. Yet this is the thesis which Dr Jantzen advocates in this book.

It is a startling thesis, but here it is argued without any attempt to be sensational or polemical. Dr Jantzen draws upon the Christian Fathers, modern philosophers and theologians, and also scientists in the development of her view. She shows throughout a sympathetic understanding of the theological tradition, and believes that to attribute a body to God is compatible with the affirmations of Christian faith, enriching them and giving them a stronger claim to be believed.

Much of the argument depends on an analogy between the being of a human person and the being of God. Incidentally, if there were no such analogy, how could we ever know anything of God, or how could God have revealed himself in a human incarnation? In particular, there is an analogy between the human experience of existing as body and soul and the relation of the physical universe to God. This analogy has been exploited by earlier theologians, such as J.R. Illingworth, but in this book it is carried further and the radical conclusions implicit in it are clearly brought out.

Modern thinking about the human being has moved away from the old dualism in which body and soul were considered to be quite different realities, mysteriously held together during the earthly lifetime of a human individual, then each going its separate way after death. Today we are more likely to think of body and soul as two aspects of the unitary reality which is a human being. The earliest Christian tradition thought in a similar way, when it looked for a resurrection of the whole person rather than for the survival of a disembodied soul.

But if we have abandoned dualism when we are thinking of finite beings, does it make sense to retain it on the cosmic level, in thinking

ix

of God and the world? It has no more plausibility there.

Of course, in speaking of the world as God's body, one must avoid the suggestion that this is to be understood in any crudely literal or anthropomorphic way. Dr Jantzen would be the first to acknowledge that much remains to be done to elucidate the idea.

The book is a model of sober restrained theological argument and makes an important contribution to current discussions concerning the central topic of theology, the being and nature of God. I count it a privilege to have this opportunity of commending Dr Jantzen's work.

Christ Church,   JOHN MACQUARRIE
Oxford

Acknowledgements

Many people have had a hand in the shaping of this book. The theme first occurred to me when I was a graduate student in the University of Calgary, under the supervision of Professors Terence Penelhum and Kai Nielsen. It was developed as an Oxford D.Phil. thesis, where I was given much stimulation and shown endless personal kindness by Professors Maurice Wiles, Basil Mitchell, and John Macquarrie. Professor Macquarrie has also been very generous in writing the foreword. The Sisters of the Love of God, Fairacres, Oxford, have been most supportive, especially Sister Josephine, who suffered many a discussion. Professor Richard Swinburne and Professor Richard Sorabji, Fr E. Yarnold and Mr Brian Hebblethwaite have offered useful suggestions for various parts. My colleagues Professor Stewart Sutherland and Mr Peter Byrne have also given helpful comments and, together with the rest of the Faculty of Theology and Religious Studies at King's College, staff and students, have made both the book and its author happier and (I hope) more balanced. To all these people, and to all my many friends and relatives who have helped in tangible and intangible ways, I offer the book itself as an expression of thanks. I wish also to thank Lesley Riddle of Darton, Longman and Todd for her interest, patience, and labour.

1

Portraits of the Invisible

The divine cannot be named . . . For no one has ever breathed the whole air, nor has any mind located or language contained the Being of God completely. But sketching his inward self from his outward characteristics, we may assemble an inadequate, weak and partial picture. And the one who makes the best theologian is not the one who knows the whole truth, for the chain (of the flesh) is incapable of receiving the whole truth, but the one who creates the best picture, who assembles more of Truth's image or shadow . . .[1]

Gregory of Nazianzus, who wrote these lines, was well aware that inevitably whatever picture we paint of God must be inadequate because it is of human workmanship. Even if the theological artist believes that his inspiration is divine, revealed from heaven, he must still portray it as best he can out of the paint box of human language and concepts: he has no other. His portrayal of God must bear some resemblance to the things we know on this earth; if it does not, it will simply be unrecognizable. The comment of Xenophanes that 'Aetheopians have gods with snub noses and black hair; Thracians have gods with grey eyes and red hair',[2] has often been taken as a criticism of religious anthropocentricity, and well it might be. But while that is a warning to be heeded, it is worth asking how the Aetheopians and Thracians might have done better. It is futile to try to escape earthly categories altogether when we speak about God: did not the Thracians do better to paint their gods with red hair, thus representing them as living personal beings whom they had to take into account, than if they had depicted them utterly without colour and without life?

One alternative might be to refuse to paint altogether, to say that God is utterly unknowable and theology is a useless effort. But if one rejects that option, if one feels that it is important to attempt to portray God, it is not possible to avoid earthly materials. And

1. Gregory of Nazianzus *Second Theological Oration* 30.17.
2. DK 21.B16.

1

the greatest artist is not the one who paints something utterly unfamiliar, but the one who portrays the familiar in a novel way, so that some aspect of its true nature is impressed upon us. The artist who paints a picture of God can give us a point of contact by using familiar, earthly imagery, and then with a few brush strokes of qualification, he can highlight the difference-in-similarity in such a way that, in Gregory's words, 'more of Truth's image' is assembled.

Obviously this does not mean that one picture of God is as good as another, any more than that one artist is as good as another. Nor can we ignore the dangers inherent in anthropomorphism. We must do our best, in our selection of earthly models, to choose the most revealing, and to consider carefully how they must be modified. Some modification is inevitable: nothing on earth is God. Too much modification obliterates the whole picture and defeats the purpose. Between these two extremes, the theologian must attempt to portray his vision of God.

But what earthly model shall he select? One set of pictures which has long dominated theological imagination is based on analogy between God and human persons which takes the relationship between God and the world to be analogous to the relationship between a human soul and a human body. When we consider how Christian theology was formed in the context of the jostling of Jewish and Hellenistic ideas in the first centuries of the Church, it is easy to see how natural a model it was. Fundamental to Jewish–Christian thinking about persons was that they were created, according to Scripture, in 'the image and likeness of God'. Plato had used the same idea, though with different connotations, and spoke of the deification of man as his chief end, a notion which the Christians modified to their own purposes: 'God made himself man, that man might become God'.[3] There were important differences between the Greek and the Jewish–Christian strands of thought, and they did not always mean the same things by the same words, but Christian Platonists like Clement of Alexandria, Origen and Augustine thoroughly intertwined them. If man is like God, on their view, then God must in some sense be like man – or at least like ideal, unfallen man – and an understanding of man

---

3. Plato *Republic* VI. 50lb, *Laws* 4.716d, *Phaedrus* 248a, *Theatetus* 176; Irenaeus *Against Heresies* V preface; Athanasius *On the Incarnation* 54; Gregory of Nyssa *Catechetical Oration* 25.
For a full discussion see Vladimir Lossky 'Redemption and Deification' pp. 97f.

2

will be a model, even if a somewhat distorted one, for the portrayal of God.

One of the Platonic doctrines often accepted by the Fathers was that whatever exactly was meant by the 'image of God', it referred to the soul or mind, not the body. Augustine wrote: 'For not in the body but in the mind was man made in the image of God. In his own similitude let us seek God; in his own image recognize the Creator'.[4] This does not mean that Augustine uniformly followed Platonic thinking in its negative evaluation of the physical: the body, created by God, is not itself evil. If it were, how could we understand the doctrines of the incarnation and the resurrection?[5] Neither is the mind a divine substance, but a created one, and whatever affinities it may have with God, it still belongs on the far side of the gulf that divides God from all created things. Nevertheless, it is not in the physical but in the spiritual aspect of man that Augustine found a model for understanding the divine Trinity, because although the image of God in man has been distorted through sin, man is still able to enter into a spiritual relationship with him,* the mind can become 'partaker of God'.[6] This granted, Augustine is able to find an astonishing range of parallels between the human mind and God, triads on the human level which mirror, more or less adequately, the divine Trinity.

Once the distinction between mind and body was drawn in this way, and the mind was identified as the bearer of the image of God, it was only a small step further to see in the relation of the mind to the body a model of the relationship between God and the world. If the real person is the soul, it can get along without the body, for instance, just as God transcends and stands in no need of the world. Although many of the Fathers affirmed a resurrection of the body, those more strongly attracted by Platonism, as for instance Origen, believed that the soul would be released from the material body — so they saw a natural parallel between the independence of the soul

4. Augustine *Commentary on the Gospel of John* XXIII.10.
5. This is masterfully presented in Margaret R. Miles *Augustine on the Body*.
6. Augustine *The Trinity* XIV.8.11; cf. Gregory of Nyssa *On the Soul and the Resurrection* 15.

---

* The use of the masculine pronoun to refer to God is for convenience only, and should not be taken to imply that God is exclusively male. Indeed as the theme of the book unfolds, it will become clear that both masculine and feminine are included in God – and much more besides.

3

from the body and the independence of God from the world.[7] (Origen, indeed, also believed that the soul pre-existed the body as God pre-exists the world, but in this the Church did not follow him.) The soul, furthermore, was thought to pervade the whole body; until Descartes connected it with the pineal gland, it was thought of not as localized at some specific point in the body but as somehow transfusing it, though essentially independent from it at least to the extent that it could survive bodily death. Thus the soul both transcends the body and is immanent in it, and so can serve as a model of the transcendence and immanence which characterize God's relationship to the world. Thomas Aquinas drew the parallel in explicit terms: '. . . we find a certain imitation of God in man . . . in that all man's soul is in all his body and again all of it in any part of the body, in the same sort of way as God is in the world.'[8] And if there is a puzzle about how an incorporeal God could exercise a causal influence on the world, one can always point to the similar interaction between the non-material mind and the material body, which, though it does not explain the puzzle, at least brings it into the realm of the familiar. Of course, that could have the opposite effect of making the mind–body interaction appear problematical too, and in due course this worry became acute, but as long as mind–body dualism was taken for granted, there seemed no reason to reject the notion that an incorporeal God could act upon the physical world.

Thus for centuries the picture painted of God and the world was a cosmic version of the picture of man conceived of as soul and body. Such a picture of human personhood, however, has been increasingly undermined as unable to cope with the combined protests of psychology, physiology and philosophy, not to mention those coming from within theology itself; and today few people would be willing to accept a view which does not take the body seriously as essential for human wholeness. But if once the dualist model of the human person is rejected, what other model can we find for trying to understand the relationship between God and the world? The gap created by a rejection of Platonic–Cartesian dualism as a theory of human persons is an opportunity for a theologian to rethink his understanding of God and his relationship to the world along more holistic lines, using a holistic model of human personhood as a basic point of departure. In the end of the day, some

7. Origen *On First Principles* 3.6.6; cf. *Against Celsus* 3.41f; 4.56f. See also J.N.D. Kelly *Early Christian Doctrines* pp. 344f.
8. Thomas Aquinas *Summa Theologiae* Ia.93.3.

4

qualifications will undoubtedly have to be made on this model too, but it will be theologically constructive to avoid making them until we are forced to do so. Thus we will see more readily what creative theological insights can be generated from a holistic model of God and the world.

A useful place to begin is to examine the theological reasons for affirming human wholeness rather than dualism. It might be supposed that the most reasonable course would be to examine the evidence from the Scriptures, to see what sort of anthropological model can be derived from them. But it soon becomes obvious that (as we really knew all along) the Bible is not a textbook of philosophy or theology but a set of accounts of individual and collective religious experiences and reflection upon them. The question of dualism is not directly tackled in Scripture, and such indirect references as there are are by no means unanimous. No purpose would be served in this context by listing all the scriptural texts which refer to souls or spirits and discussing their interpretation with respect to the question of dualism: it is easy to find some which have a decidedly dualistic ring, but just as easy to find others which do not.

Nevertheless, although the language and concepts used in the biblical texts are by no means uniform, there is a growing consensus among biblical scholars that the Hebraic concept of humanity which pervades the Old Testament and is a dominant force in the New is a holistic one. Hellenistic thought tended to separate man into an inner psychic component and a non-essential physical body, but the Hebrews thought instead of a psychosomatic unity. Various organs of the body were particularly significant for specific psychic functions: the heart, the kidneys and the bowels were each the seat of important emotions, and the body was thought of, not as a habitation in which we dwell or an object which we use, but essential to ourselves and necessary for finding and expressing meaning in our lives.[9] This does not mean that the Hebrews were materialists in the reductionist sense in which that word is understood today. There was, in their view only a single reality, not two separate ones; yet that reality could not be adequately described in material and mechanistic terms but must also take into account the psychological, sociological, and especially spiritual dimensions of personhood. The significant fact is that for the Hebrews the whole person, including

9. Cf. W. Eichrodt *Theology of the Old Testament* Vol. 1 pp. 131–50; also Gerhard von Rad *Old Testament Theology* Vol. 1 pp. 152–3.

the body, is above all related to God and to the community; it is this psychosomatic unity which is the human person.

This holistic view of personhood which biblical scholars suggest on the basis of textual studies is very much strengthened by more broadly theological considerations. Indeed, it is implied in some of Christianity's central doctrines: creation, sin and salvation, and eternal life. It will be worth while to examine each of these in turn.

Whatever we make of the story of creation as given first in Genesis and then in various ways throughout the Bible, two things stand out. First, God is in some sense the origin of all that exists, and hence of the material world; second, in consequence of this the material world cannot be called evil. In the first chapter of Genesis God rejoices over his creation and sees that it is good. He takes pleasure not only in the beautiful environment into which humans are about to be installed, but most of all in the man and woman themselves: God declares the whole to be very good. It is noteworthy that the two living beings made, respectively, from clay and from a rib, are said to be made in the image and likeness of God. When we look carefully the context does not bear Augustine's view that the image of God is to be found in man's mind rather than his body: in Genesis it is explicitly the joint reality of male and female in relation to God which is said to be in God's image. Whatever exactly is involved, the physical (and indeed sexual) aspects cannot be excluded. A Christian anthropology therefore begins from the position that persons are created and affirmed by God as embodied human beings, not as souls imprisoned in an alien body from which they yearn to escape.[10]

It has sometimes been thought, however, that such a holistic view as is implied by the doctrine of creation breaks down when the notions of sin and salvation are considered. Historically, this has taken two forms. The first is the allegation that sin occurs when the soul falls prey to the passions and evil desires of the body: the material part of the person is the cause of all the trouble. On this view, salvation is the freeing of the soul from the evil demands of the body, and the ultimate hope is for incorporeal immortality. This might be the view of a superficially Christianized Socrates in Plato's *Phaedo*, for example: salvation comes by release from the body, so the lover of wisdom lives even now with 'one foot in the grave' – as ascetically as possible.

The other form of arguing for dualism from the doctrines of sin

10. Cf. Karl Rahner *Foundations of Christian Faith* pp. 27–30.

and salvation is to urge that it is the soul itself which is sinful. The body is of little consequence and can – perhaps must – be ignored. Did not Jesus say that it is not what a person eats or drinks that makes him unclean, but 'what comes out of the mouth has its origins in the heart; and that is what defiles a man'?[11] Even those sins whose outward manifestations are necessarily physical, such as murder and adultery, are thus sins of the soul. Consequently it is our souls that must be saved; not, this time, by release from our bodies, but by radical forgiveness, cleansing and renewal. Salvation is an inward and spiritual matter; our bodies are inconsequential. If the former view has certain affinities with Plato, this one bears comparison with certain of the Gnostic sects described by Irenaeus, who, according to him, believed that if the spiritual man was saved, his bodily activities did not matter.[12]

When the arguments are stated crudely in this way, it is easy to see their shortcomings, even if one still wishes to affirm the need for radical forgiveness and renewal. But their real failure is not the inadequacy of their presentation, but rather their misapprehension of the concepts of sin and salvation: when these are more clearly understood, they point towards a holistic anthropology. The word 'sin' is used in Scripture with a far more basic meaning than 'illegal' or even 'morally wrong' actions. It means, rather, missing the mark, falling short: in the words of the writer to the Romans, 'All have sinned, and come short of the glory of God.'

But what does it mean to come short of the glory of God? It can hardly mean that sin consists of being human, having a body rather than being divine or disembodied, for sin is related to moral responsibility and hence to that over which we can exercise a choice. What, then, is the glory of God of which man has fallen short? Again Irenaeus provides insight: '. . . the glory of God is a living man; and the life of man consists in beholding God . . .'[13] To be fully alive, to come to complete fulfilment of our personhood – this, according to Irenaeus, is what God glories in, and this is his intent in the creation of persons. Sin, then, is acquiescence in anything which falls short of this complete fulfilment. And since we all do fall short, and find ourselves unwilling or unable to develop fully as we ought, salvation involves the accepting and forgiving grace of God manifested in Jesus Christ which progressively frees us from all that is less than being fully alive, less than complete fulfilment

11. Matt. 15:18–20 NEB.
12. Cf. Irenaeus *Against Heresies* I.6.2.
13. Ibid., IV.XX.7.

7

in continuous self-transcendence to the 'vision of God' of which Irenaeus speaks.

But complete human fulfilment is fulfilment of the body as well as of the mind – or, better, fulfilment of the whole person, not split into mental and physical segments. The actualizing of one's human potential is an actualizing of one's whole self in relation to God; reducing the idea of fulfilment of the person to fulfilment of the mind is excessively rationalistic. Human development undeniably requires *ascesis* – bodily training – so that the body does not become the master of the self; but training is not expurgation, and does not imply that the body plays only a negative role in human fulfilment. There is nothing new in this; the New Testament writers were well aware of the physical dimension of sin and salvation. They encouraged their readers to present their whole selves to God, including their bodies, and they spoke of sexual fulfilment as a model of the fulfilling relationship between Christ and the Church, a model that could hardly be used if the physical were worthy only of condemnation.

A profound deepening of the concepts of sin and salvation is provided by H.D. Lewis in the form of abbreviated suggestions at the end of his defence of dualism, *The Elusive Mind*. Professor Lewis shows how sin consists essentially of improper absorption with ourselves, while redemption means freeing ourselves from this self-preoccupation through love initially received from God and passed on to others. The lostness and helplessness of our time is reflected, he says, in contemporary literature, absorbed with unreality and emptiness and 'soul-destroying guilt'.[14] He then states that this can be best understood if we recognize the ontological reason for the inwardness and elusiveness of the self – that is, if we adopt a dualist perspective.

But why should this be so? We can wholeheartedly agree that his analysis of 'the wages of sin' is one aspect of missing the mark: instead of developing into a loving, caring person one becomes absorbed in one's own soul. Thus redemption is a liberation, a release from this self-preoccupation, whether this preoccupation concerns itself with one's sin or one's sanctity. Yet all this is also true in a holistic framework. The soul or self in which we become absorbed is not some ontologically discrete part of the person, as we can see when we consider how often self-preoccupation is connected with sexual preoccupation. Thus Professor Lewis's

14. H.D. Lewis *The Elusive Mind* p. 327.

comments concerning sin and salvation, perceptive as they are, lead us away from the dualistic perspective which he wishes us to adopt. The Christian understanding of the life to come further affirms an essential wholeness of personhood. The whole person is created by God, the whole person sins, and the whole person must experience the salvation and liberation which ultimately results in eternal life. Although there has been a steady stream in Christianity which has spoken of incorporeal immortality, it is significant that the creeds themselves never once mention the soul. The future hope is expressed in the phrases, 'And I look for the resurrection of the dead, and the life of the world to come.'[15] Exactly what form this resurrection is to take is another question, and one about which there is continuing speculation. But if the logic of the anthropology so far presented is to be carried through, the one option that is not open is to affirm disembodied existence as the state of ultimate completion of a human person. If salvation applies to the whole person, then it must also apply to the whole person when it is extended into the future.[16]

Thus a Christian doctrine of persons requires, in its key affirmations of creation, sin, salvation, and the future state, an anthropology which accepts the body as an aspect of total personhood. Radical dualism and a denigration of the physical is not an option for Christian theology. Because of this, it cannot be used by a theologian as a model for the relationship between God and the world. On the other hand, a whole new creative possibility is opened for theology when a holistic model of human personhood is explored. If human personhood and particularly the relationship between the mental and the physical in human persons is still to provide an analogy for the relationship between God and the world, as I shall suggest that it does, the analogy will no longer point towards a God existing independently of the world and interacting with it like a majesty from on high, because we can no longer think of our souls, the analogate, as being essentially different from our bodies and ruling over them. Rather, the relationship between God and the world will be much more intimate, and his attributes of power and knowledge will not be forces externally applied, as we shall see.

Two notes of caution must be sounded. The first is, simply, that this should not be taken as a philosophical refutation of dualism. For that, much more would be required, especially in the light of

15. So the Nicene Creed. The Apostles' Creed says simply, 'I believe in . . . the resurrection of the body and the life everlasting.'
16. Cf. Karl Rahner *Foundations of Christian Faith* p. 434, 182.

9

contemporary presentations of dualism such as that of Professor Lewis cited above. My main objective is not to mount a full-scale attack on dualism. Instead, I am beginning from the position that, rightly or wrongly, I like many others find dualism inadequate philosophically and psychologically as a theory of human persons. Yet it is often believed that although dualism is philosophically problematical it is theologically indispensable, and thus a theist is committed to its defence whether he likes it or not. The above comments are intended to show that in terms of human persons this is not so: theological anthropology can be holistic in its approach. The remainder of the book is devoted to showing that, when the same holistic approach is applied to our understanding of the relationship between God and the world, it frees a theist from defending on theological grounds a dualist ontology which he otherwise finds wanting, and furthermore offers insights into God's relationship with the world which provide much-needed balance to contemporary theology.

The second note of caution is that we should not assume that there is no further use for the distinction between the material and the spiritual. Oscar Cullmann once pointed out that the Jewish Scriptures, for all their holistic anthropology, insist on a distinction between what is merely physical and what is an aspect of the inner or spiritual life of humanity, and designate these by the terms 'body' or 'flesh' and 'soul' or 'spirit' respectively.[17] Similarly in the tradition of Christian spirituality there is a use for the concept and vocabulary of soul as distinct from body; we would only be impoverished if we were to dismiss the writings of the great mystics and spiritual writers as gibberish whenever they speak of the purification and illumination of the soul. Insights and methods of such spiritual giants as Mother Julian of Norwich and Walter Hilton do not become irrelevant just because we need a new vocabulary to avoid dualistic anthropology: people did not stop warming themselves before fires when they found themselves required to think in terms of oxidization rather than the release of phlogiston.

Nevertheless, although there is a legitimate use for the terms 'soul' and 'spirit' and indeed a great demand for deepened appreciation of the 'spiritual' writers, the soul–body distinction finds its proper place only when it is made within the context of a holistic anthropology. The primitive concept is the concept of a person; notions

17. Oscar Cullmann 'Immortality of the Soul or Resurrection of the Dead?' pp. 24–5.

of souls and bodies are derivative from that basic concept rather than the other way around.

2

Icon or Idol?

In the preceding chapter we saw that Christian anthropology points us in the direction of a holistic concept of human personhood rather than a dualistic composite of body and soul. It follows that, if the relationship between God and the world is to be understood as analogous with the relationship between a person and his or her body, then the God–world relationship is a much closer one than we might have guessed from the monarchical cosmic dualism which formed so large a part of the traditional belief of the Church, and a major task of theology will be to try to understand this relationship in a way that does it justice. But the theological reverberations which this would generate are dependent on that rather large 'if': it is important to see why our notion of personhood is so significant for our understanding of God.

We agreed at the outset that whatever picture we paint of God must be painted with earthly materials and from earthly models; but we also saw that it would have to be qualified in important ways. Nothing on earth is God or could be God; consequently any earthly model comes up against limitations in its attempt to symbolize God, and can at best partly reveal and partly conceal him. A picture of God may be an idol or an icon, depending on how we respond to it. If its inherent limitations are forgotten, it is inevitably the former. It is patently absurd to suppose that we could exhaustively symbolize the ultimate; at best, we can paint an icon which will mediate some aspects of its reality to us. But, as Paul Tillich insists, if any symbol or icon, no matter how profound, becomes absolutized, as though it were itself ultimate rather than the means through which the ultimate is revealed, idolatry has taken place. Each symbol, each icon, should therefore carry with it a reminder that it is no more than symbolic, that it points to the ultimate without being ultimate itself.[1] The question which faces

---

1. Paul Tillich *Dynamics of Faith* p. 97; see his *Systematic Theology* Vol. 3 p. 206. See also Shubert Ogden *The Reality of God* p. 49.

us, then, is the extent to which personhood can be a symbol of God, and how far it has to be qualified.

There are two ways in which the model of human personhood can be qualified to illuminate our understanding of God, both of which, I suggest, are important, and both of which can be carried too far, so that the model is obliterated altogether. The first begins by asking whether Christian anthropology can really serve as a model for theology proper: to what extent can we legitimately proceed from a doctrine of man to a doctrine of God? Even if holism is necessary in our understanding of human persons, this can only be extended to God if we grant that God is a person too. But can we do this? Is he not rather the Ground of all personhood and all being, the Absolute? Is it not unduly restrictive to think of him as a person?

The second sort of qualification is less radical. Even if we grant that God is personal, that human personhood requires embodiment, and that divine personhood is in some respects analogous to human personhood, how far can the analogy be extended? God must after all far transcend our human characteristics or he simply would not be God. Therefore if we use human embodiment as a part of our understanding of God, we shall have to qualify the model in such a way that it is illuminating for our understanding of God; if we take it over too simplistically we shall have turned the icon into an idol. The way to proceed here is directly dependent upon what we make of the former qualification. When we understand more clearly how the notion of personhood applies to God, we shall be in a better position to see how a model of embodied personhood can provide new insights, and in what ways it must be restricted.

When we look, then, at the question 'Is God a person?' we find that to answer it we shall have to say what we mean by 'person'. The word is used ambiguously, even within Christian doctrine, as reflection on the theology of the Trinity shows. We speak of the Trinity, sometimes, as three persons in one Godhead; but the Church has often insisted that this does not mean that God is a sort of committee composed of three members who always think their thoughts simultaneously and are unanimous in their decisions. Christianity is monotheistic, not tritheistic. The origin of the word 'person' as used in the doctrine of the Trinity has little to do with the concept of 'discrete individual'; rather, it is closely related to the idea of 'dramatis personae' – manifestations or roles played by a Unity. Its primary sense was originally the mask which an actor wore to signify his role; from there it came to stand for the actor

13

himself, but not for his self-consciousness or 'real' self, but for his dramatic self – who he was in the play.[2] It was the contention of the Arian heretics, not of the orthodox, that Christ was a different 'person' from the Father in a sense more nearly like our current use of the word: the Church, on the other hand, insisted that he was 'of the same substance' as the Father.

But it is one thing to damn a position as heretical; quite another to solve the problems which gave rise to the heresy. The perplexity of the Arians is still with us: if the unity of the Godhead is so strongly stressed, how is it possible to affirm that God was incarnate in Jesus of Nazareth without lapsing into patripassionism – a notion which the Church also declared heretical? On the other hand, the doctrine of the Trinity arose out of a monotheistic faith precisely because Christians so strongly believed that the life of Jesus of Nazareth and the coming of the Holy Spirit were manifestations of divinity which could not be adequately accounted for in any other way. When the line was drawn between what was God and what was not God, Christ and the Holy Spirit had to be included in the former category, not the latter. But given that this is true, we would naturally expect that the persons of the Trinity would after all be distinguishable in a tritheistic way – and so we have come full circle. G.W.H. Lampe's diagnosis of what most of us do when we try to think about the Trinity is that, rightly or wrongly, we usually do not take the word 'person' to mean simply 'manifestation' but rather something more like 'individual centre of consciousness' – which we then quickly repudiate when reminded of its tritheistic implications.[3] The variety of ways in which the doctrine of the Trinity has been interpreted illustrates admirably the ambiguities surrounding the word 'person' when applied to God.

Karl Barth, in his profound reflections on the nature of God as personal in the Trinity, uses Buber's distinction between 'I' and 'It' to illuminate what we mean by affirming that God is personal. Because of the puzzles which arise from the ambiguity between 'person' understood as a centre of consciousness opposed to 'person' understood as a divine 'I' (not a divine 'It'), the concept of God as *a* person, let alone as three, is highly debatable for trinitarian theology. But although we may on these grounds be hesitant about saying that God is a person, this should not be construed in such

---

2. See J.N.D. Kelly *Early Christian Doctrines* p. 115; G.L. Prestige *God in Patristic Thought* pp. 157f; Jaroslav Pelikan *The Emergence of the Catholic Tradition (100–600)* pp. 172f.
3. G.W.H. Lampe *God as Spirit* pp. 226f.

14

a way that we consider God to be somehow less than personal. God confronts us as a 'Thou', not as an 'It'.[4]

If we accept the more general formulation, we can steer away from further questions about the individuation of persons and the puzzles of the doctrine of the Trinity, and focus our attention instead upon the characteristics of personhood upon which, after all, the analogy to human persons depends. Our glance at the puzzles of trinitarian doctrine has already been useful in this connection, because it has made us aware of two aspects which we normally consider essential to personhood: consciousness, and contrast from 'Its' – inanimate things. Our everyday idea of personhood expands this considerably. It involves the capacity to think and feel and love, to make moral decisions, to act and to reflect, to laugh and cry and communicate with other persons. If any of these capacities are missing from an entity, we may say that it is not personal – perhaps it is an animal, or an inanimate object. Alternatively, in the case of severely retarded or comatose human beings, or the humanoids of science fiction, we are sometimes inclined to say that personhood has either never developed at all or that it is severely attenuated.

Now these capacities which we consider to be integral to personhood are routinely ascribed to God by both Scripture and tradition. They may stand in need of considerable refinement and qualification when they are applied to God; many writers insist on this. But it remains true that, although God is the supreme mystery, and hence all our predicates stand in need of qualification in their application to him, he is a personal mystery, not less. He is the One who acts on the world and interacts with humans freely, graciously, and intimately. Some of the ways in which this personal action is described in biblical and post-biblical writings may well be intended metaphorically, enabling us to see what God is like and how he acts by analogy with characteristics and actions of human persons. When Moses commemorated the deliverance of Israel from the pursuing Egyptian hosts, he sang,

> Thy right hand, O Lord, glorious in power,
> Thy right hand, O Lord, shatters the enemy . . .
> At the blast of thy nostrils the waters piled up,
> The floods stood up in a heap . . .
> Thou didst stretch out thy hand,
> The earth swallowed them.[5]

4. Karl Barth *Church Dogmatics* Vol. I Part I pp. 351f.
5. Exodus 15:6–12 RSV.

Not even the most literal-minded believers think it necessary to hold that the writer meant that God literally has nostrils through which he puffed and blew until he made the water stand up 'in a heap'. But even if talk about nostrils should not be taken literally, the writer's main point is to praise the Lord's mighty activity on behalf of his people. This affirmation – and indeed this incident – became the focus of a major theme of Jewish theology: God has a direct control upon the world, including, should he so wish, the ability to intervene miraculously in earthly affairs.

Christianity, like Judaism, accepted this principle as essential. In recent years the idea that God's agency could ever be correctly characterized as supernatural intervention has been called into question: not only those sceptical of religion, but theologians themselves are having to ask what sense it makes, in an age of technology, to assert that God can directly interfere with natural processes and causal sequences.[6] But orthodox belief through most of the history of Christianity has held firmly to the doctrine of divine agency, providential and miraculous, so at this stage we will ignore latter-day puzzlement, reserving it for further consideration later on.

In any case, when biblical writers said that God's right hand brings about their deliverance, it is not likely that they thought, at least after a certain stage in their religious development had been passed, that God literally has a right hand. But they certainly did mean that God literally can and will direct the affairs of this world in such a way that his people will be directly benefited: he delivers them from their enemies – or delivers them to their enemies to teach them a lesson, he provides for their needs, he gives them special tokens of his favour. Scripture relates numerous incidents in which this direct influence upon the natural order was of a miraculous kind: the sun stood still in answer to Joshua's prayer, the Lord sent a fiery chariot for Elijah's personal conveyance, God prepared a vine to grow up over the head of his pouting prophet Jonah and then sent an east wind to cause it to dry up and die. And even if these stories are deliberately mythological in character, the myths would lose their point if the activity of God in earthly affairs was denied. In short, according to Christian thought rooted in Jewish Scriptures, God's personal nature is revealed through his personal activity. He can intervene in the affairs of the world if he wants to, and sometimes he does just that.

6. See Maurice Wiles 'Religious Authority and Divine Action'; Gordon Kaufmann 'On the Meaning of "Act of God"' in his *God the Problem;* Brian L. Hebblethwaite 'Providence and Divine Action'.

16

Furthermore, this divine activity is linked with divine self-communication: it is a gracious intimacy, not an anonymous interference. The Jewish prophets ring with the phrase 'Thus says the Lord', and the point of God's action in allowing distress, punishment and captivity is drummed home: God wants the loyalty and love of his chosen people. Indeed, it is not too much to say that this intimacy and self-communication lies at the very heart of Christian belief. Christianity might well be thought worthless if it is not at its centre a personal relationship with God, out of which all its actions flow. The primary commandments of this highly personal religion are 'Thou shalt *love* the Lord thy God . . . and thy neighbour as thyself', commandments which can be better understood as breathtakingly gracious permission than as 'laws' to be submissively obeyed. Theology could hardly be Christian unless it recognized as fundamental the personal nature of God. This is part of the point of Karl Barth's comment that 'the doubtful thing is not whether God is person, but whether we are';[7] it is from his wholeness and love that personhood is derived.

Barth reminds us that, in the encounter with God as person, we encounter God as incomprehensible: we must not forget God's inconceivability while dwelling on his intimacy. Nevertheless, the most exalted pictures we can paint of God, the ones given to us most consistently in Scripture and tradition, are pictures conveying a deep sense of personhood: Creator, Lord, King, Spouse, and, above all, Father. The real question therefore becomes not whether personal qualities and characteristics can be attributed to God, but whether the concept of God is so rich that the phrase 'God is personal' shuts us away from the wealth of God's being rather than exposes us to it. And this, indeed, is a question worth pondering. We have already considered the words of Gregory of Nazianzus that God himself is beyond naming: it is for that very reason that we are engaged in the search for a picture which will enlighten us rather than mislead.

There has been an influential strain in Christian theology which has denied the very possibility of such a picture: any image is inevitably idolatrous, and must be shattered. The *via negativa*, well trodden by spiritual giants from the Pseudo-Dionysius to Thomas Merton, exists precisely because of the awareness that God, who is so much greater than our concepts of him, cannot be known with

---

7. Karl Barth *Church Dogmatics* Vol. I Part I pp. 138–9; see also Karl Rahner *Foundations of the Christian Faith* p. 74.

our meagre intellects, but can only be apprehended by the 'sharp dart of longing love', which alone is capable of piercing the cloud of his glory.[8]

One of the philosophers who has drawn attention most forcefully to the inadequacy and deceptiveness of 'person language' in describing that which transcends all language is F.H. Bradley. He argues that, when theists wish to ascribe a personal nature to God, they do so because of the normal finite connotations of the term 'personal': they want a God who loves them, listens to them, responds to them, in the way that a Father or a good friend does. Yet Bradley points out that, with the other side of their mouths, theists wish to say that God is infinite, immutable, and beyond time; and that not infrequently they could be convicted of indulging in a surreptitious slide between the two sorts of language, a slide disguised by the words 'infinite person', which are in reality nothing but two sides of a contradiction. Bradley sees this as just disreputable:

> Once give up your finite and mutable person, and you have parted with everything which, for you, makes personality important. Nor will you bridge the chasm by the sliding extension of a word. You will only make a fog, where you can cry out that you are on both sides at once.[9]

There is something in this accusation of double-dealing, even if it has not been quite such deliberate fog-making as Bradley's words suggest. He is certainly right when he says that a large part of the motive for saying that God is personal is to affirm that he has real relations with us, analogous to the relationships between finite selves: we have already seen that this is true. It is also true that theists have not always been as careful as they ought to be with tricky words like 'infinite' and 'immutable': we shall have to consider these later on. Bradley, however, takes a radical line. He rejects the idea that the Absolute is personal, in the finite sense of the term. The Absolute rises above all such characterizations. Nevertheless, he says, this should not be taken to mean that the Absolute is impersonal: that would be an equal and opposite error. The Absolute, rather, transcends distinctions like personal and impersonal altogether; though if one or the other must be chosen,

---

8. See *The Cloud of Unknowing* by an unidentified early English mystic; Dionysius the Areopagite *The Mystical Theology* pp. 195–6; Thomas Merton *Seeds of Contemplation* p. 29.

9. F.H. Bradley *Appearance and Reality* pp. 471–2.

it would be better to think of the fullness of the Absolute in personal than in impersonal terms. Best of all, however, is to call it 'super-personal'.[10]

It is a moot point, surely, whether Bradley's concept of the Absolute really provides a higher synthesis of various apparently antithetical notions, or whether it is itself merely a catchword that enables him to hold simultaneously to both sides of a contradiction in just the same way as he accused theists of doing when they speak of an 'infinite person'. Nevertheless, his conclusion is not altogether repellant to Christian doctrine. Everyone agrees that God's reality goes beyond anything that we can say about him; even those who find the *via negativa* too dark and gloomy a road to do justice to the light and joy of the gospel would still recognize that our minds can at best give us only a dim picture of the beauty and reality of God. Here we see 'through a glass darkly'. So when we say that God is personal, we do not thereby say that he is *only* personal, or think that we have fully described him, any more than when we call him Father we thereby exclude his motherhood.

The trouble is that when we insist on how far God transcends out little categories, we sometimes quite illogically slip into thinking that their inadequacy makes them false. We must be on our guard against supposing that, because personal categories can never exhaust God's reality, he is somehow *im*personal: without doubt he is more, but not less, than personal. Thus although the model of God based on human persons will undoubtedly need to be qualified in important ways, it is the best model we have. We can be quite sure that, although the God whom Jesus worshipped goes beyond the highest personal categories that we could ascribe to him, he certainly does not fall short of them.

If human persons are icons of God, however, in the sense of pointing towards his personal nature, this brings us to the second sort of qualification that we noted at the beginning of this chapter. It has regularly been held, even by those who have accepted that God is personal, that the analogy to human persons collapses just at the point where we begin to speak of embodiment: this is a significant respect in which God goes beyond our humanity. I have suggested, on the contrary, that the picture of God which emerges if we begin with the holistic model of humanity is an enriching one for theology, and that although the notions involved in embodiment require qualification for their application to God, they are more

10. Ibid., pp. 472–3.

illuminating than those which take the model of the relationship between God and the world to be a dualist conception of humanity.

The balance of this book will be devoted to showing how this is so – how far we can press the claim that God's relationship to the world is analogous to the relationship between a person and his or her body when this latter relationship is understood holistically. It is of course no secret that traditionally this approach has been vehemently rejected, and it is important to see why. The Fathers of the Church were intent on preserving some important religious and philosophical doctrines which they felt would be sacrificed if God had a body or was embodied in the world. It is therefore significant for us to discover what these doctrines were, and then to see how the new model of an embodied God retains what is religiously and philosophically important in them.

3

Theological Tradition and Divine Incorporeality*

In the previous two chapters we have seen, first, that Christian anthropology points in the direction of a holistic concept of human personhood, and second, that any theism which can be called Christian must take seriously the personal nature of God, otherwise it forfeits its claim to follow in the steps of the one who staked his life on his right to call God 'Father'. But this leaves still unanswered the question of how the personhood of God can be analogous to human personhood and in what ways it must be qualified. Because of this, it is now important to turn to traditional theology, to try to uncover and make sense of some of the basic reasons why it has been held so firmly that God could not be embodied, and what significant doctrines the Fathers were trying to conserve by this claim.

The idea that God is not embodied has been the stock-in-trade of theological orthodoxy for so long that it comes as a surprise to find that 'from the beginning it was not so'. In the first efforts towards theological understanding in the patristic period, the Fathers of the Church were divided on the question of whether or not God was embodied. Some of them, like Tertullian, perhaps influenced by the Stoics, clearly thought that he was.[1] Irenaeus is less explicit, but the idea that God has a body could easily be taken as the logical consequence of his line of reasoning. In his discussion of the notion of the image of God in man, he does not relegate this image to man's reason (nous) as the Alexandrians and Augustine were to do, but rather implies that the image of God is to be found in the body of man: this then becomes part of Irenaeus' understanding of the salvation and ultimate resurrection of the whole person, not just the soul.[2]

It was possible for some of the early Fathers to take this approach because, as Origen noted, Scripture is not explicit: nowhere in the

---

* In this chapter I have drawn heavily on G.W.H. Lampe *A Patristic Greek Lexicon,* especially listings under *asomatos* and its cognates.
1. Tertullian *Against Praxeas* 7.
2. Irenaeus *Against Heresies* V.6.1.

21

Bible are we told that God is incorporeal. Origen himself believed that the Scriptures had other names for it, and indeed he thought that incorporeality could be predicated not only of God but also of Christ, the Holy Spirit, the angelic hierarchies, and all rational souls.[3] But anyone who does not share Origen's philosophical presuppositions might well remain unconvinced if he restricted himself to quoting texts from Scripture, since a great many of these, referring to God as Father, King, Leader, Judge, Shepherd, and so on, would suggest, if taken at face value, that God is indeed corporeal.[4] It is only after divine corporeality has been ruled out on philosophical or theological grounds that other interpretations (figurative, allegorical, instances of theophany, etc.) are found for passages which at first sight seem to indicate an embodied God. Although there is much variety in Scripture, including considerable refinement towards nonanthropomorphism within the biblical tradition itself, many biblical passages can be found which, if taken literally, point towards corporeality.

Scripture does say, of course, that God is Spirit (*pneuma*). But *pneuma*, in the Greek text of that time, did not necessarily indicate incorporeality as we would expect; in fact, it was sometimes taken to imply the reverse. We can observe this in the Stoic philosophy of the time, where *pneuma required* corporeality. According to Stoicism, God and the world are composed of the same stuff. The creative fire which rules the universe is the *pneuma*: some Stoics, like Cleanthes, took this to be the sun, but even those who doubted this did not think that *pneuma* was a mental or spiritual substance of a kind somehow different from matter.[5] In the light of this, the remarks of Origen, who was commenting on John 4:24 in opposition to their teaching, are less startling. He says that, although some would argue on the basis of this verse that God has a body, such an argument would be mistaken because in this case the word *pneuma* must not be taken in its physical sense but in a way more suitable to spiritual understanding.[6] It is evident from this remark that one very natural interpretation of the word *pneuma* to the

3. Origen *On First Principles* Preface 9.
4. See James Muilenberg 'Is There a Biblical Theology?' p. 33.
5. See Philip Hallie 'Stoicism' pp. 19–22; J.M. Rist *Stoic Philosophy;* F. Copleston *The History of Philosophy* Vol. I Part 2, Chapters 36, 39, 40.
6. Origen *Commentary on the Gospel of John* xiii.21. See also his *On First Principles* I.1.1. In this connection it is also worth pondering what Paul might have meant by his remark in connection with the resurrection of the dead that 'if there is such a thing as an animal body, there is also a spiritual body'. 1 Cor. 15:44 NEB.

reader of the New Testament in Origen's time might not have been 'incorporeal' but the very opposite.

The Fathers responded in a variety of ways to Stoic thought, and felt themselves at liberty to draw upon some aspects of their teaching while repudiating others. On the whole, Stoic influence on Christian ethics was greater than Stoic influence on Christian metaphysics with its monistic understanding of reality. As the Fathers were inclined to interpret it, Stoic monism entailed materialism and determinism, and was thus incompatible with Christian teaching. And in their dismissal of Stoic ontology, they dismissed the idea of an embodied God. The fact that other Greek philosophical schools from the earliest times had also been unwilling to divide reality between the corporeal and the incorporeal only served the Fathers as a reminder of the fallibility and futility of human philosophical speculation. John Chrysostom and Tatian, from very different positions in the theological spectrum, agree in their scornful attitude towards philosophy in general and the notion of a corporeal God in particular.[7]

From anti-philosophical attitudes such as theirs, drawn from such different sources, we might have expected the Fathers to stay clear of philosophical speculation and content themselves with preaching the gospel. But this would have been impossible. Theological understanding (which must underlie any gospel preaching) cannot take place in a vacuum; it always builds within a metaphysical framework, even when that framework is not wholly conscious and even though it modifies the framework in the process. Even the Fathers who railed against Athens and tried to turn their faces resolutely towards Jerusalem could not help but be influenced by the thought forms of their day. But not all the Fathers thought that philosophy should be repudiated. Some of them, from Justin Martyr onwards, were well pleased to turn philosophy to their service, and to make out of a duly Christianized Platonism a powerful metaphysical framework for their theology.

According to a Platonic system of thought, it would be utterly inconceivable that God should have a material body. For a Christian Platonist, the idea of divine corporeality could be dismissed by a simple syllogism:

God is supremely Real and supremely Good.
Matter is least real and least good.
Therefore God must be immaterial.

7. John Chrysostom *Homilies in John* 66.3; Tatian *Oration to the Greeks* 25.

The syllogism is simple, but the underlying metaphysics is not. To understand the argument and the reasons why the Fathers adopted it, it will be helpful to explore the Platonic conception of Reality and its implications for theology.

It is well known that one of the legacies of pre-Socratic philosophy to the great Athenian thinkers was preoccupation with change. Yet change itself is parasitic on permanence: something which changes must still be the same thing, otherwise we would not have change but succession: it is only because a person continues to be the same individual as he or she passes from youth to age that we can speak of him or her changing. Thus permanence must be the basic underlying structure of reality, even though transience is the most striking fact of our experience.

But when Being (permanence) is thus seen to be the basic framework and Becoming (transience) is secondary to it, it is easy to attach a higher value to permanence than to fluctuation, especially when human experience of the latter involves loss, ageing, and death. It would hardly do to say that God is transient or fluctuating: he is faithful and enduring for ever, 'without shadow of turning'. Thus the biblical teaching of the steadfastness and unchanging purposes of God was crystallized, by the Christian Platonists, into a doctrine of divine immutability. God is Being – Supreme Reality – and is thus contrasted with change, Becoming. But it is obvious that matter – physical bodies – is subject to change. Hence, by contrast, if God is immutable he must also be immaterial; and Fathers like Athanasius were not slow to draw the conclusion.[8]

The transience experienced by man as a member of the world of Becoming is distressingly noticeable in three particular respects: his subjection to fluctuating passions, his physical decline manifesting itself in daily need of sleep and rest and ultimately in old age, and finally the transience of life itself and the certainty of death. God, however, is subject to none of these changes, and since all of them are linked to our corporeal nature, corporeality and mutability form an obvious contrast to divine incorporeality and immutability. Methodius of Olympus and later Gregory of Nazianzus stressed how God's immunity from passion, suffering and weariness sets him apart from any human experience.[9]

But if God is associated with the concept of Being rather than Becoming, and is thus immutable and indestructible, he must be

8. Athanasius *Defence of the Nicene Definition* III.10.
9. Methodius of Olympus *Discourse on the Resurrection* III.XIX; Gregory of Nazianzus *Second Theological Oration* 28:VII; John of Damascus *The Orthodox Faith* I.4.

eternal: his 'years have no end.' Now the Platonic idea of eternity was not an idea of unending duration, but of being outside time altogether. Time is only the 'movable image of eternity',[10] and although it is part of our experience of this fluctuating world, true Being is immune not just from the ravages of time but from time itself. This was also incorporated into patristic theology. Gregory of Nyssa thought it obvious that not only was God not subject to time, but time flowed from God; he was the Creator who had laid time and space 'as a background to receive what was to be; on this foundation he builds the universe'.[11] Thus past, present and future necessarily belong to everything within the order of creation, but to God everything is equally present 'as in an instant'. One of the interesting features of Gregory's account is his linkage of time with space. This is an early instance of a model that was to become prominent, in which time was pictured spatially: the universe is spread out in time just as it is spread out in space. Perhaps one of the reasons for this is that time is measured by the movement of spatial objects. In the *Timaeus*, for example, immediately after the comment that time is 'the movable image of eternity' there is a discussion on the motions of the heavenly bodies by which time is measured. Thus time, change, death, space and matter are drawn together into a web, and over against them is God, timeless, immutable, indestructible, and incorporeal.[12]

Once these contrasts between Being and Becoming, God and the world, have been drawn, it is a very small step to make further distinctions and parallels. First, since Being is that which is permanent and is basic to the very possibility of change, Being must remain unitary while change takes place. But obviously, *many* changes can happen to a single thing: changes of colour, shape, size and texture all affect a single primrose in its brief history. Thus Being, the underlying permanence, might be said to be single, One, while the multiplicity of changes constitutes the Many. Secondly, the changes and chances of this passing world, the everlasting impermanence and flux, since it has already been contrasted with true Being, can be taken as Appearance only, not as Reality. Reality is One, it is true Being, immutable, eternal and incorporeal. It is

10. Plato *Timaeus* 37d.
11. Gregory of Nyssa *Against Eunomius* I.26; see also Augustine *Confessions* XI.13; Boethius *The Consolation of Philosophy* V.6; Anselm *Proslogium* XIX; Thomas Aquinas *Summa Theologiae* Ia.X.
12. See Augustine *The Trinity* XV.4.6; also Adolf Harnack *History of Dogma* Vol. 2 pp. 204–6, 350.

not Becoming, the Many, the dance of shadows on the cavern of our sense-perception.

Clearly, such a position will have to be modified before it can be incorporated into Christian theology, since in Christian thought other things besides God (human persons, for instance) are genuinely real. But then, the same could be said of Platonism. Plato and his followers did not say that all the things we experience are unreal. It is rather that their reality must have some source other than themselves, and thus they are real, not of themselves, but by participation in the source of their reality. A painting, for instance, may be genuinely beautiful – its beauty is real enough – but its beauty is a participation in the Form of the Beautiful. If the beauty of the painting were taken by itself, without acknowledging its source, this would be highly misleading, for in itself it is more akin to appearance than to reality. But if the beauty of the painting is recognized as a participation in Beauty itself, the Form of the Beautiful, then it can correctly be said to be real, though with a derived reality. Thus in the absolute sense, Reality is One: there is only one ultimate source of reality, and the Many are real only by participation in it.

Now this line of thought was clearly congenial to Christian theology, which was anxious to affirm that all things owe their very existence to the creative will of God. Although many things besides God are real, their reality is derived, not innate. If they are taken as real in themselves, not in the context of their dependence upon God, they are radically misunderstood: the appearance has been made a substitute for the reality rather than a signpost towards it. In the ultimate sense, only God is real, he alone is uncaused. Interpreted in this way, as for instance by Clement of Alexandria,[13] Greek philosophical ideas about the One and the Many, Appearance and Reality, could be pressed into the service of Christian doctrine without compromising the reality of the world and its contents while still insisting that this reality is derived, not innate.

When Clement comments on the notion of divine Being, it is interesting to note that he inserts a phrase about divine incorporeality. This is wholly in line with Platonic thinking about the relationship between Reality and the appearances which we experience. Reality is not accessible to our senses, gripped as they are by the fluctuation of the passing show, but to our intellects. The light of Reason persuades us of the illusoriness of our physical perceptions: the contrast between Being and Becoming, Reality and Appearance,

13. Clement of Alexandria *Fragment from the Book of Providence.*

finds a correlative contrast between reason and sense-perception.[14] This is why the Fathers needed to insist on God's invisibility. That which is corporeal, and is hence accessible to sense-perception, is only a shadow of Reality, not its substance. Any admission that God was visible would therefore be tantamount to an admission that he was less than ultimate Being. This is foreign to our own way of thinking, since our world view is shaped by scientific presuppositions which encourage us to think that reality is paradigmatically perceptible, and any non-perceptible entity can have at best a derived reality by being somehow hooked into the empirically observable: the logical positivists gave this view forceful philosophical articulation. But the Fathers who followed Platonic teaching held the precisely opposite view. Reality is ultimately spiritual as opposed to material, and cannot be reduced to this passing world which, imprisoned as we are in our bodies, traps us into its idle show. Release comes, before death, only by training ourselves to look with the eyes of our minds rather than those of our bodies, for 'the things which are seen are temporal, but the things which are not seen are eternal' (2 Cor. 4:18).

So although we might have thought that it would be difficult to know God because his invisibility and inaccessibility to our senses would to a certain extent remove us from direct knowledge of him, in a Platonic scheme of thought just the reverse is true. A thing is intelligible not in so far as it is available to our senses, but in so far as it is available to our minds. As Socrates had said when instructing his disciples on knowledge of the Forms, the body, far from being a help in this quest, is a perpetual distraction; the way to success is to apply 'pure and unadulterated thought to the pure and unadulterated object'.[15] Only a spiritual world could be accessible to the mind; thus if we are to hope for any knowledge of God at all, he must be incorporeal.[16] In this way the incorporeality of God becomes the metaphysical requirement for any spirituality or mysticism, and

14. R.E. Allen *Plato's 'Euthyphro' and the Earlier Theory of Forms* p. 68. But for an alternative view, see I.M. Crombie *An Examination of Plato's Doctrines: Plato on Knowledge and Reality* pp. 319f.
15. Plato *Phaedo* 65d–66a.
16. See Origen *Against Celsus* VII.38. See also Eusebius *The Oration of Eusebius in Praise of Constantine* IV. This does not mean that the Fathers (or their Platonic philosophical mentors) thought that God could be completely known: on the contrary, he far surpasses our knowledge. But this is because he is more than we could know, not less, as he would be if he were material. See Frances Young 'The God of the Greeks'.

asceticism – freeing oneself from the tyranny of the senses – is a prerequisite to spiritual insight.

But it not just that *we* can know God because he is incorporeal; God himself can know, in a way which would have been impossible for him if he had had a body, since matter impedes knowledge. God, thus, is essentially intelligible nature – all knowing. When the Christian belief in a God whose understanding is infinite and who has numbered the very hairs of our heads encountered Greek thought about the essentially intelligible nature of the non-material, it was natural for the two to coalesce into a doctrine of divine omniscience rooted in divine incorporeality.

Related to this is the understanding that the real essence of anything is not in any sense its material structure. Matter is only the receptacle for reality, passively receiving whatever forms 'enter into her and go out of her.'[17] To be sure, we never perceive unformed matter; we perceive bodies of one sort or another. But it is the form which makes the thing to be what it is, the form is the intelligible essence. Matter as such could have been made into any shape or body – it could have been anything. Matter itself is unintelligible and unknowable and wholly potential, whereas form is incorporeal and knowable. A body is formed matter, and thus it is knowable in its essence, but yet changeable. It is amenable to sense-perception, yet its reality lies in its form which can only be truly grasped by the intellect. Thus Plato speaks of three kinds or levels of being: forms, which are eternal and immaterial, bodies, which are formed matter, and matter, which is unformed, unknowable, and without beginning or end.

Now, clearly, Christian theology could not adopt these statements without qualification, since it could accept neither the incorporeal eternal existence of uncreated forms, nor a belief in ultimately independent matter: all things owe their existence to God. But once this important qualification had been made, the idea that bodies are a conjunction of form and matter was accepted and had a long and significant history in Christian thought. In spite of their recurrent complaint that it is in just such philosophizing that heresies have their roots, it is clear that the Fathers drew upon a Platonist metaphysical structure quite as much as did the heretics, with the important caveat that God is the absolute creator of all things.[18] And some of them, of course, were happy about this borrowing of

17. Plato *Timaeus* 50c-52b.
18. Hippolytus of Rome *Refutation of Heresies* 1.16; Augustine *City of God* VIII. 11.

philosophical framework. Augustine went so far as to wonder whether Plato's doctrines in the *Timaeus* might not have been influenced by Hebrew Scriptures, even if only through an intermediary interpreter, so congenial did he find them. Ultimately, Augustine had to part company with a Platonic account, because he could not give up the doctrine of creation *ex nihilo*. Even then, however, he interpreted the chaos spoken of in Genesis 1 as the unformed matter, the receptacle for the forms, thus coming as near as possible to the teaching of the *Timaeus*.[19]

There are significant differences between a Platonic and an Aristotelian understanding of matter and form, but both agree that matter is potentiality and that it is the conjunction of form and matter that results in a body. Thomas Aquinas, influenced by both philosophical strands, draws them together into an explicit argument against the idea that God could have a body. God as the creator must be utterly 'actual', that is, without any potentiality – or in other words, without matter.[20] Because matter is utterly inert, essentially lifeless, and is passive to all change, divisibility and restructuring, having no power of its own or any self-direction, and no capacity for consciousness, it is the very antithesis to God who is the living God, eternal, immutable, self-directing, all-powerful and all-knowing. Thus for Aquinas and many others with him, incorporeality was indispensable to any concept of God; it is indeed the central fact about him on which everything else depends. To question it is tantamount to questioning whether God – a living God – exists at all. This is the force behind Aquinas's words, 'In this way . . . God and prime matter are distinguished: one is pure act, the other is pure potency, and they agree in nothing.'[21] Since the central contention of Christian theism is that there is a God who is alive, active and personal, a holistic model of man could hardly have been imposed upon this metaphysical framework, either in our understanding of human personhood or for its divine analogate.

Several other issues flow out of this immediately. In the first place, the Fathers emphasize the finitude and limitation of any material body, contrasting it with God's infinity and omnipotence: no limits can be put on God, nor can he be bounded in any way. Methodius of Olympus, in his discussion of the origin of evil, rejects

19. See John Goheen *The Problem of Matter and Form in the De Ente et Essentia of Thomas Aquinas* p. 43; Augustine *Confessions* XII.8; Plotinus *Enneads* II.10.
20. Thomas Aquinas *Summa Theologiae* Ia.3.1.
21. Thomas Aquinas *Summa Contra Gentiles* I.17.7.

the view that matter is coeternal with God: it is created by him, and to that extent, contrary to Platonic thought, it is good. Nevertheless he rejects as preposterous the very idea that God could be in any sense material: this he sees as utterly incompatible with divine limitlessness and power.[22] Thus Methodius, along with other Fathers, couples God's greatness and lack of limitation with his independence of matter. God is sovereign, God is in control; there can be no entertaining of the thought that God is part of the seething fluctuation of materiality. He rules over this ocean of change; he is not himself floating in it.

Similarly, the fact that God is incorporeal and thus utterly unlimited and unbounded by spatial configuration was felt to be congenial to the doctrine of divine omnipresence. Since God is not restricted to any place, the way a material body must be, he can pervade all. The doctrine of omnipresence is juxtaposed with the doctrine of incorporeality in two slightly different ways. Some of the Fathers see God as essentially outside of all the physical world, but omnipresent in virtue of his omnipotence and omniscience. Thus Clement of Alexandria writes, 'In substance far off (for how can the originate come close to the unoriginate?) but most close in power, in which the universe is embosomed.'[23] This idea should not be taken to imply a spatial contrast between God and the world, since Clement has expressly ruled out such spatial categories by insisting on incorporeality. The distinction, rather, is between the essence of God, which Clement, perhaps in an effort to avoid pantheism, contrasts with the material world ('in substance far off'), and God's activity, which is to be felt throughout the universe. The whole line of thought can be seen as an attempt to articulate a doctrine of (Stoic) immanence without sacrificing (Platonic) transcendence thereby lapsing into (Stoic) pantheism – a classic example of the way the Fathers took various strands of contemporary thought and wove them together into their own design.

Others of the Fathers, however, thought rather of permeation: God is everywhere literally, not only in power and knowledge and goodness but in substance. This was modelled after the manner in which the human soul was thought to permeate the whole of the human body without being localized in any part of it, so that, for

22. Methodius of Olympus *On Free Will* 5.6. See also the comments of G.L. Prestige *God in Patristic Thought*.
23. Clement of Alexandria *Stromaties* 2. See also Clement of Alexandria *Fragment;* Athanasius *Defence of the Nicene Definition* III.11; Theodore of Mopsuestia 'On the Incarnation VII'.

instance, the entire soul occupies an injured finger – but if a finger on the other hand were also injured, the whole soul would occupy them both simultaneously. This idea that God is literally present everywhere in his fullness is distilled in Thomas Aquinas's teaching that God exists in everything by power, presence and substance, thus knowing and causing all.[24] The varying nuances of the doctrine of divine omnipresence and their implications for immanence and transcendence will occupy us further on, when we see how these are illuminated by a holistic model; the present point, however, is that either form was assumed to turn on the doctrine of divine incorporeality.

Platonist philosophy could supply a useful web of concepts for making sense of divine immanence and transcendence. Plato's post-ulation of 'two worlds', and sophisticated Christian Platonist thought which drew on him, was not (in spite of the way it has sometimes been taken) an attempt to postulate a spiritual world somewhere in space (heaven) which was an ethereal reduplication of this material one. The Forms, it is true, exist seperately from the things which, by participating in them, are their shadows or images in this world of sense-perception. And their existence is a real existence; that is, the Forms are not, according to Plato, merely a reification of our collective subjective abstractions. But it must be remembered that they are spiritual realities, not material ones; so that, although they are real, they do not have *any* spatial location, even though in another sense they pervade all things and things derive their reality from participation in the Forms.[25]

This relationship between the reality of the transcendent Forms and their immanence in the material objects which participate in their essence could be neatly appropriated by the Fathers, who held that God was both the transcendent Creator and giver of all reality, and also that he preserved and sustained all things by his pervading presence and power. Thus where later theologians have sometimes seen immanence and transcendence as in tension and difficult to reconcile with one another, the Fathers, basing all on a doctrine of divine incorporeality, thought of them as complementary concepts. God can truly be immanent and pervade all precisely *because* he is transcendent and incorporeal.[26]

The comparison of the relationship between soul and body with

24. Thomas Aquinas *Summa Theologiae* Ia.8.3.
25. See F. Copleston, S.J. *The History of Philosophy* Vol. 1 Part 1, p. 200.
26. Gregory of Nazianzus *Second Theological Oration* 28.8. The scripture reference is to Jeremiah 23:24.

that between God and the world was thus a useful way of understanding how God could on the one hand be utterly different from
the world, and yet, on the other, not be utterly cut off from it because
of the difference of substance. This was of enormous importance
to the Fathers.[27] But there are some additional aspects of Plato's
metaphysics (or at least, their interpretation of it) which the Fathers
found congenial, and when these are combined with the above
understanding of transcendence and immanence we see even more
clearly the centrality of the doctrine of divine incorporeality in the
whole web of Christian metaphysics.

The spiritual world of Plato's Forms is arranged hierarchically,
with each reality deriving its being from that which stands above
it, so that the most real is at the summit. Individual Forms, though
sui generis in themselves and in that sense not definable, may be
defined in terms of higher Forms in relation of species to genus. In
the *Meno*, for instance, various virtues are recognized as all being
species of the genus 'virtue', though the genus remains as yet unspe-
cified. But if the Forms are to be defined in this way, then the
spiritual world cannot be a Platonic flatland; it must be a 'tiered
universe.'[28] This hierarchical ranking could be usefully adapted to
theological purposes. Matter, as pure potentiality, was lowest on
the scale of reality for both Plato and the Fathers. Formed matter
– that is, physical objects – would be higher; this, indeed, is the
lowest level of reality that we ever experience, since we never could
encounter primordial matter in itself. Next would come physical
objects infused with soul, like ourselves, and above us are ranks of
angels, who are composed of spiritual substance and form. All of
these derive from God, who is thus at the farthest extreme from
matter in this 'great chain of being'.[29]

But this 'tiered universe' is, in Plato, not merely an ontological
hierarchy but also a moral one. Plato gave a special place in the
spiritual world to some of the Forms, which were then seen as
equivalent (or nearly so): Beauty, Goodness and Being. In the
famous myth of the cave, the Form of the Good is likened to the
sun; it is that by which all things are seen and from which, ultimately, they have their being. And in the *Symposium*, the philosopher

27. Eusebius *Oration in Praise of Constantine* XII; Gregory of Nyssa *Against Eunomius*
    XII.1. The scripture reference is to Col. 1:16–17.
28. See R.E. Allen, op. cit. pp. 90–102; F.M. Cornford *Plato's Theory of Knowledge*.
29. For a fuller history of this idea, see Arthur Lovejoy *The Great Chain of Being*. He
    also shows how the Platonic and Aristotelian traditions were blended in this
    concept's history.

aspires to the vision of Beauty itself, which is described in a burst of poetry like the ancient choric odes, but in terms which make it clear that, far from being in competition with ultimate Reality and ultimate Good, the Form of Beauty is at one with them.

The identification of Beauty, Goodness and Reality into a single supreme principle was carried forward in the Platonic tradition in a somewhat modified form, which made it even more congenial to Christian thinkers. Plotinus, reflecting Aristotelian influence, places supreme Reality, which he calls the One, outside the chain of being altogether. Strictly speaking, in the Plotinian system the One is beyond being, beyond goodness and beauty, beyond any predication whatever. Yet although in that strict sense nothing can be said about the One, it is right for us to think of the One as the Good and the Beautiful – this is certainly far nearer the truth than its unqualified denial would be. The Form of the Good, which for Plato was the supreme Form, has been exalted in Plotinus to a status above any of the Forms, which in his system emanate from it. In Plotinus as in Plato, the Forms comprise the highest realm of Being, but in Plotinus the source of this Being, the One, cannot itself be Being, but must transcend it. It is not difficult to see in Plotinus's characterization of the One parallels to Christian statements about God, including the warning, noted in the previous chapter, that ultimately God transcends all human predication. Thus the themes of his Being (Being beyond Being), self-sufficiency, simplicity and perfection become pivots of Christian theology, as for example in Anselm's formulation of the ontological argument or Thomas Aquinas's discussion of divine unity in the *Summa*, not to mention the mystical theology of the Pseudo-Dionysius and his heirs.

We can thus see that the background against which the doctrine of divine incorporeality was formed could hardly allow an alternative. The web of concepts was tightly drawn, each idea connected to the others. In the Platonic tradition, with its conjunction of the source of Being with ultimate value, to see which is the soul's highest knowledge and perfect beauty, we have the framework within which the Christian Church could build her metaphysical theology, moral theory and mystical teaching. And this framework, put to such powerful use, had as one of its central features a dualist anthropology which modelled the relationship between God and the world. Hence in that context, it would be unthinkable to ascribe any sort of material body to God. To do so would be, in that framework, to impute to him only derived reality, remove him from the uppermost place in the ontological and moral hierarchy, and make him less knowable and less worthy of knowing.

However, the metaphysical structure in relation to which Christianity was formulated no longer commands the respect it once did. The idea of a hierarchy of being and goodness does not comport at all well with modern philosophical ideas about what a fact is and its relation to value, and the notion that an invisible entity, in no way perceivable by the senses, is more accessible to knowledge than a material object of which we can have sense data sounds foreign indeed to our ears. And, as we have already noted, the dualist anthropology which provides a crucial model for the formulation of the God–world relationship, is giving ground in modern thought to more holistic concepts of personhood.

Nevertheless few, even when they would reject these elements of Platonic thought, have questioned the doctrine of divine incorporeality, or explored the theological possibilities inherent in a holistic model. Instead, there has been widespread concentration on what could be meant by the doctrine that God is an incorporeal personal being, one who communicates and acts on the world, but who is 'spirit' – that is, bodiless. The question has been forcefully raised whether such a conception is even coherent. One would not need to accept all of Harnack's claims to recognize that there is truth in his contention that the personalistic emphasis of Jewish and early Christian thought cannot be superimposed on to Hellenistic metaphysics without generating enormous tensions. And many philosophers of the twentieth century doubt whether incorporeal personhood is a defensible concept, especially now that dualism has no wide acceptance as a theory of human personhood. Yet both attackers and defenders of theism regularly assume that the doctrine of an incorporeal God is essential to Christianity; thus there is broad agreement that, if the concept is indeed incoherent, Christian theism has been radically undermined. Understandably, therefore, a considerable amount of energy has been poured into both the attack and the defence of the concept of incorporeal personhood.

But it seems to me to be at least as important to re-examine the whole assumption of incorporeality and its metaphysical web. The difficulties generated by a doctrine of incorporeal personhood are so severe that it is worth asking ourselves whether the model of human personhood, which is our best model of God, might not provide more creative insights if we took seriously the holistic nature of the model: perhaps our theology could be illuminated if we came to a revised understanding of God: God embodied. Theology can get along a good deal better than most theologians would guess with the claim that God is embodied, as I shall try to show. This, then, is important both for its own sake, in terms of the theological insights which it yields, and as a reply to those who, like Kai Nielsen, argue that the idea of an embodied God is just false, while the idea of an incorporeal God is incoherent.[30] Perhaps the whole attack and defence of theism revolving around questions of incorporeality is misconceived and unnecessary, and a picture can be painted, using a holistic human model, which 'assembles more of Truth's image'.

I wish, therefore, to pull at some strings of the metaphysical web in which the doctrine of divine incorporeality has been traditionally entangled. Our look at the Fathers in this chapter has shown us what that web is. It has also shown some important aspects of our understanding of God which the adoption of that metaphysical system was meant to safeguard: his limitlessness, omnipotence, omniscience, and omnipresence, his changelessness, indestructibility, and eternity, his transcendence and immanence, his supremacy as Creator of the world and hence the source of all its reality, goodness, and beauty, and his accessibility to his creatures so that, finite though we are, we can in some frail measure truly know God. Any toying with theological metaphysics cannot afford to forget these themes, and if the Platonic metaphysics is rejected in favour of a holistic model, it will be important to elucidate and where necessary qualify this model, so that philosophical and religious adequacy is enhanced rather than undermined.

30. Kai Nielsen *Scepticism* p. 10.

4

God, Time and Space

In the Bible, there is a strong emphasis on the eternity of God. He is not an idol with a temporal beginning and subject to possible destruction, he does not become weary or grow old, his years have no end. God is the God of the living: indeed, he is often called YHWH – interpreted as 'I Am' or 'He who is'. Given the modified Platonic structure of metaphysics within which the Fathers formulated their theology, it was perhaps inevitable that this biblical teaching of divine eternity should be interpreted not simply as everlasting duration but as timelessness: God as pure and permanent Being utterly transcends the world of Becoming and its mutability. True Being cannot be adequately described in tensed language.

Following Plato's teaching that Being itself could not be temporal, Augustine, whose thoughts on divine eternity were to have enormous influence on the shaping of Western theology, thought of time as an entity – that is, as something created by God which did not exist until God made it. Others had asked what God did before he created the world; but Augustine dismissed the question as resting on a misunderstanding. If time itself is created by God, then there is no such thing as time before creation, and hence the question, resting as it does on the temporal notion 'before' cannot arise. Thus according to Augustine, God's eternity is not to be interpreted as endless duration through time, but as timelessness. God, as maker and master of time, is outside of time altogether.[1]

This theme is taken up repeatedly by the medieval theological masters. Sometimes God is spoken of as the 'Eternal Now', sometimes, incompatibly, as utterly outside time. The former view might seem natural if one began by thinking in terms of God's constant and unchanging presence. But many theologians believed that even those considerations needed to be transcended, since if God is the maker of time, then he must be outside *all* time, even 'now'. Boethius

---

1. Augustine *Confessions* XI. 13. See also *City of God* XI.21.

gave this view its classic and often-repeated expression: eternity is the 'simultaneously whole and perfect possession of interminable life',[2] and the word 'perfect' is specifically intended to eliminate the 'now' of time.

Nor is the doctrine of divine timelessness restricted to medieval Roman Catholic theologians. In more recent times, Schleiermacher insisted, in somewhat Thomistic fashion, that God is entirely outside time. According to Schleiermacher, we must not fall into the trap of speaking of God as having endless duration, for endless time is quite a different concept from eternity. If we mentally translate the concept of eternity as 'everlasting', we completely fail to do it justice, because we then make the existence of God a temporal existence, even if one without limits. One cannot make eternity out of time by the simple expedient of cutting off both ends.[3]

If this understanding of the doctrine of divine eternity is accepted, we might well ask whether it has implications for the spatial relationship between God and the universe. Clearly, the notions of space and time are very closely linked, as has become increasingly noticeable in modern physics. Hermann Minkowski, a leading exponent of the impact of the theory of relativity on our notions of space and time, goes so far as to say: 'Henceforth space by itself and time by itself, are doomed to fade away into mere shadows, and only a kind of union of the two will preserve an independent reality.'[4] If this is true, then we might well wonder what implications a holistic model of God would have on the doctrine of divine eternity. If God is timeless, must he not also be spaceless, incorporeal? On the other hand, if we begin from a holistic perspective, what sense can we make of eternity?

Einstein and his fellow physicists were, of course, not the first to reflect on the correlations between space and time; indeed, their interrelationships are embedded in our common language. Time is often spoken of in spatial terms, as though the universe is spread out in time just as it is spread out in space. We speak, for example, of a 'long' time, a 'short' time, and even a 'space' of time. One of the most important spatial metaphors for time is direction. Space is three-dimensional, with the three pairs of directions length, breadth and height. Time is often thought of as one-dimensional, with the single pair of directions past-future. Both time and space

2. Boethius *Consolation of Philosophy* V.6.
3. F. Schleiermacher *The Christian Faith* 52.2. See also Thomas Aquinas *Summa Theologiae* I. 10.4.
4. H. Minkowski 'Space and Time' p. 297.

can be specified in terms of their relationship to some standardized point of reference: for spatial location one can refer to one's position relative to the equator or the North Star; for temporal location to an event like the birth of Christ. But there are also puzzling asymmetries between the notions of space and time. One of the most striking differences is that, within limits, one can easily travel in any spatial direction, but one cannot 'move about in time' in any analogous way. It is quite simple to return to the *place* where I was on my sixteenth birthday, but I cannot return to that *time:* time, as we say, has 'moved on' and there is no going back. For that matter, it is just as impossible to travel into the future at will: I might long for my holidays to come, but nothing I can do will transport me to that time. The time will come, but I cannot go to it. And when it does come, it will, disconcertingly, be present – and indeed all too quickly past – no longer future. We cannot literally enter the future at all.

These pre-scientific puzzles about the disanalogies between space and time are perhaps the germ of a new series of metaphors of time as a great sea upon which we sail – the ocean of time – or else as a stream which flows over us, who are always in the present, in its relentless transition from future to past. Sometimes the metaphor is reversed, so that the transition is from past to future: age, memories and experience increase as the past develops into the present towards the future. These ideas of the flow of time, and the various ways that we can speak of it, have been labelled 'the myth of passage'.[5] It is a myth, in the pejorative sense, because it rests on a confusion. Movement, change or flow is itself temporal; motion and time are not separable. But if we were to speak of *time* flowing, then this movement of time would have to take place relative to some 'hypertime'. We can grasp this by considering the idea of speed. If we ask, for example, how fast a hawkmoth can fly, the answer is something like fifty kilometres per hour. But now suppose we ask how fast time flies. It is impossible to give any answer at all, unless the utterly useless one that one hour takes exactly one hour to pass. We could only give an answer about the rate of change in terms of time, and therefore cannot use the same sort of language to try to describe time itself, unless we postulated a 'hypertime' – but this would then stand in need of just the same sort of elucidation which we now feel it necessary to supply for the concept of time,

5. J.J.C. Smart 'Time' in Paul Edwards, ed. *The Encyclopedia of Philosophy* Vol. 8 pp. 126–34.

and so would not have been of any use. The conclusion to which this drives us is that time itself cannot be said to change: things change, and their changes can be temporally measured and located, but it makes no sense to speak of a temporal movement or location of time itself.

These puzzles about time and change are augmented by reintroducing the concept of space. Anything spatial can in principle change (or be changed). It can change in terms of its external relationships with other spatial objects, and it can change in its internal relations too, by being divided, for instance, or, in the case of persons, by going through conscious processes. Now since change is a temporal process, anything spatial must be temporal. This means that if we use a holistic model of God, and thus think of God as embodied (in a sense still to be elucidated) and therefore spatial, he must also be temporal; conversely, if he is timeless, he must be incorporeal.

Great problems are generated by the claim that God is timeless, from which a holistic model of God can liberate us. For if God is timeless, he must also be immutable; and if he is absolutely changeless, it is hard to conceive of how he could relate to the spatial and temporal world. Of course, those who spoke of God as timeless were aware of these difficulties, and proposed various means of dealing with them. Aristotle, who put the problem into the frame of reference which it would subsequently assume, thought that reflection on the nature of time showed that any doctrine of creation – as well as any doctrine of an end to the world – was impossible. His argument was that it is inconceivable that time should have a beginning, because, for any postulated beginning, we can always ask what happened before it – thus seemingly referring to a time before the beginning of time. But time, he believed, was essentially linked to change, in such a way that, if there were no change, there could be no time either. Now if change (motion) is eternal, then there must always have been something that moves or changes. There must always have been a world (though of course it need not have been like the world we know), and by the same token, there can never cease to be a world.[6]

This was all very well for Aristotle, who was not on other grounds committed to a doctrine of creation, but it posed enormous problems for the Christian philosophers and scientists who followed him. As we have already seen, Augustine wrestled with the problem of the relationship between time and creation, and found it necessary to

6. Aristotle *Physics* 251b 10–13.

insist that time itself is a part of that creation: God is timeless and the maker of time, and therefore although it seems to make sense to ask what God was doing before the creation of the world, in reality this question is misguided. Its apparent meaningfulness is a function of the inescapable temporality of our own life and psychological structure, but in this case our finitude leads us to deception. Thus although Aristotle is right to say that the idea of a beginning of time is inconceivable, this inconceivability is, according to Augustine, psychological, not logical. Time itself was created by its master, a timeless God.

Thomas Aquinas keenly felt the pressure from both Aristotle and Augustine. He recognized the need to say that God created time and is himself timeless and immutable, yet he also recognized that ascribing the inconceivability of a beginning of time to our human weakness does not adequately resolve the problems. The logic of the concept of an event requires that there must be a 'before' and an 'after' – this is not just a function of our psychology, as Augustine had thought. Aquinas accordingly drew the distinction along different lines. He said that there is a difference between real time – the time of the world – and imaginary time, which is the time we can conceive of. Although we can conceive of time before the creation of the world, this time would only be imaginary, not real. Real time began with the beginning of motion of created things.[7]

But there is an insuperable difficulty with this view: no further account can be given of this postulated imaginary time. The essence of real time is tied up with the movement of created things, and cannot be understood apart from it. But how are we to understand imaginary time? By definition, it has nothing to do with change or motion – but then why should we call it time at all? From the account Thomas has given us, we can say nothing whatever about it, and it is hard to see how it solves the problems for which it was introduced. We would still have to account for how God is related to this imaginary time. Did he create it too? If so, the problem begins all over again.

Both Augustine and Aquinas kept within the general framework set by Aristotle's account of time; in particular, they both accepted his premise that time and motion are essentially linked. But the Newtonians called this premise into question. Newton distinguished between relative space and time, which we measure by means of

---

7. Thomas Aquinas *Commentary on Aristotle's Physics* IV.17.577; also VIII.2.990; cf. his *Commentary on the Metaphysics of Aristotle* XII.5.2498.

the motions of bodies, and the more fundamental absolute space and time, which are infinite and not essentially linked to motion, but can and do exist perfectly well where nothing whatever moves. Time and space in this absolute sense are receptacles, containers of the events and objects which fill them. On this view, time itself could not be said to change: it is infinite and the 'place' of the succession of things.

But Newton was no atheist, and believed in the doctrine of creation. How could his views be squared with such a doctrine? Only by a radically different conception of the relationship between God and the world. Augustine and Aquinas had a 'monarchical' view of God: he is 'out there', timeless, spaceless and changeless, essentially other than the world. Newton, however, made the suggestion that the relationship is much closer. God, omnipresent in both space and time, 'constitutes duration and space'[8] – time and space are aspects of the deity, at least in the sense that God wholly permeates the infinite containers, time and space, which are substantial entities. Thus the world was created in time and space, but time and space are themselves infinite and uncreated. Creation took place at a moment in time; but time itself existed, infinite and unoccupied (except by God) before that moment. On Newton's view, God could scarcely be thought of as timeless or spaceless, though clearly he could be omnitemporal and omnipresent: indeed, it would make sense to say that time and space are manifestations or perhaps even attributes of God.

Leibniz sharply criticized Newton's ideas of absolute space and time, and argued that time must after all be related to motion. There can be no such thing as empty time. We can, of course, conceive of something happening before the creation of the world, but strictly speaking this means only that we can conceive of a possible world which existed before this actual world. This possible world contained the imagined event. Such an exercise in imagination is by no means equivalent, Leibniz urged, to thinking of empty time, time before any world at all. Indeed, Leibniz considered that his view was necessary if we are to be able to find any sensible answer to Augustine's puzzle about why God created the world when he did and not earlier – an insoluble dilemma if one accepted Newtonian accounts of space and time. For Leibniz, God would be temporal if he changed in any way (for example, if God had thought

8. Isaac Newton *Philosophiae Naturalis Principia Mathematica*, General Scholium to Second Edition.

41

processes, or if he responded to the events of the world); but if God were utterly immutable, he would also be timeless. Since the orthodox view was that God indeed is immutable, Leibniz's concept of time would be compatible with the doctrine of divine timelessness where Newton's theories would have more difficulty.

Yet it was Newton, not Leibniz, whose views about the nature of space and time dominated subsequent science, whether or not those views were heterodox. If God *constitutes* space and time, then it seems difficult to escape the conclusion that he is in some sense the container of the universe and all its events. But he would then be neither timeless nor immutable, for every change in the universe would be a change in God. This position, however, would be uncomfortable for traditional theology, and an escape was provided by Kant. Unlike Leibniz, Kant accepted the force of Newtonian science and saw at once its greatness and its challenge. The system he developed was intended to take Newton seriously, and also to show the limitations of his position, by the expedient of distinguishing the world as we perceive it and the world as it really is – the phenomenal and the noumenal world. The world as we perceive it is indeed characterized by infinite time: contrary to Leibniz, empty time is conceivable. The reason for this, however, is not to be sought in the objective structure of the real world. Rather, time, like space, is a sort of grid which we place upon all our perceptions: the framework we impose upon the world. Whether the real world is temporal or not we have no way of knowing: certainly its temporality does not follow from the fact that we cannot help but perceive the world in this way, because this is a fact about us and our inevitable contribution to perception, rather than a fact about the world.[9]

Now, if this is the correct understanding of space and time, then there is no obstacle to the belief that God is timeless, even if Newtonian physics reigns supreme in the phenomenal world. God is not part of this world. But space and time cannot apply to absolute reality, which can never be empirically known. Thus it is possible to maintain *both* that God is timeless and incorporeal, *and* that space and time are infinite with respect to empirical 'reality' – the phenomenal world which we experience through our senses.

But this Kantian medicine may be even less acceptable than the ills which it is meant to cure. In the first place, the distinction between the real (noumenal) world, about which we can know

9. Immanuel Kant *Critique of Pure Reason* Transcendental Aesthetic II.4.2&6.

nothing, and the world we empirically discover has been vigorously attacked by philosophers from Kant's time to our own; yet unless this can be upheld, and with it Kant's ideas of space and time as our subjective contributions to perceived reality, the problems about God's relation to space and time are unresolved. And philosophical considerations apart, there are theologically unhappy consequences. If Kant is right, then God is neatly banished to the noumenal world, and out of the world of our experience. We can know nothing about this noumenal world, nor is it at all clear that a member of the noumenal world (if it is proper to speak of it as having membership) could act upon the world of our experience. Kant himself is aware of this, and consequently thinks of God rather as a necessary postulate for ethics than as a personally active being with whom humans can communicate or to whom they can relate; in *Religion Within the Limits of Reason Alone* he shows that the whole point of religion is to provide a stimulus for morality and a motivation to overcome moral failure. Whatever aids this is to be preserved; anything else is destructive superstition. Kant can thus retain the doctrine of the transcendence of God over space and time, but at the cost of transforming personal religion into morality – touched by as little emotion as possible.

One of the developments which a Kantian system helped to foster was a split between metaphysical speculation and empirical investigation. Philosophers could and did go on speculating about the Absolute, Kant's noumenal world, but scientists were free to ignore their pronouncements and continued to investigate the nature of space and time in the empirical world. If the results of these investigations were theologically unpalatable, one could always say that they applied only to appearances, not Reality. In the long run, however, such a division of labour becomes impossible to sustain. Whatever the excesses of the positivists and their anti-metaphysical entourage, they at least made the point that a world of Absolute Reality, utterly divorced from our experiences, is a world which literally cannot affect us in any way and about which we can know nothing. But then why bother about it? Reality in the common-sense meaning of the term is vitally involved with what we experience. Even if the positivists went too far in their link-up of meaningfulness with sensory verification, it was a natural enough over-reaction against an idealist philosophy which seemed bent on metaphysical speculation without regard for the findings of the developing natural sciences.

Meanwhile, those sciences were investigating further the relationship between time and space. In 1887 A.A.Michelson and E.W. Morley devised and conducted an experiment intended to confirm Newton's ideas of absolute space and time – and it failed. This led to a radical rethinking of fundamental Newtonian notions, especially the idea of simultaneity. Einstein argued that there could be no way of establishing that two events which are spatially separate are temporally simultaneous unless we can first establish that two spatially separate clocks are synchronized. But because there is an upper limit on the velocities of the signals we can use to co-ordinate these clocks (namely, the speed of light), this is impossible. Therefore we could never have recourse to absolute space or absolute time; space and time are relative to one another and cannot properly be treated separately. As Minkowski had shown in 1908, it was possible to construct a four-dimensional geometry in which three dimensions represent space and the fourth represents time; a line on such a geometrical graph will represent the world-line (spatial and temporal) of an object. It was this, and its applicability to theories of relativity being developed by Einstein and others, that led Minkowski to the statement already quoted, that henceforth space and time must always be considered together.

I said earlier that it is not quite accurate to say that a doctrine of divine timelessness and a doctrine of divine incorporeality stand or fall together if the theory of relativity is accepted, and we can now see why this is true. As already noted, anything spatial must be temporal; relativity theory here confirms our unsophisticated reflections. But it is not necessarily the case that anything temporal must be spatial. Time is more basic than space. For instance, the theory of relativity does not of itself solve the problem of whether disembodied persons are possible, persons who, if they had conscious processes (and if they did not, could they be called persons?) would clearly be temporal even though *ex hypothesi* not spatial. The theory of relativity applies to the relationship and measurement of space and time in the physical contents of the universe; it does not address itself to the question of whether non-spatial entities might exist, nor whether they would be temporal or non-temporal if they did. Given the relativity of space and time, it might not be possible for us to *measure* the temporal duration of a non-spatial entity or event, but this is not the same as saying that whatever is temporal must be spatial.[10]

This survey of the high points of the history of scientific thought

10. *Contra* A.R. Peacocke *Creation and the World of Science* p. 79.

about the concepts of space and time must be paralleled by theological reflection on its implications for the doctrine of divine eternity. Much work has been done in recent years on the meaning of scriptural references to time and eternity, and how the concepts of the biblical writers compare and contrast with the various strands of Hellenistic thought. Biblical writers frequently use the words αἰών and αἰῶνες, often translated 'eternal'. This in itself, however, does not tell us very much, since we still need to discover whether 'eternal' is to be understood as 'timeless' or as 'omnitemporal'. On the basis of lexical studies, it has been argued that the word αἰών should usually be translated simply as 'age' – that is, it is a precisely limited duration of time. In its plural form, it can be an expression of unlimited and incalculable duration – a plurality of 'αἰῶνες' reaching forward without measure, everlastingly. If this is correct, then, it is argued, biblical writers who used the terms usually translated as 'eternity' were very far from speaking of timelessness. Rather, they meant the whole of time, everlasting time.[11] Thus the proper understanding of the doctrine of divine eternity would be omnitemporality; when we say that God is eternal, this is equivalent to saying that God endures for ever, throughout time.

But this is too short a way with the evidence from the biblical writers. James Barr, in his study of biblical time-words, has pointed out that philosophical conclusions must not be read directly off simple lexical data. In the case of words for time and eternity, it is necessary to examine the total context in which the words are used, lest we attempt to wring out of the biblical writers answers to questions which we, not they, are asking. In particular, from the fact that a word obviously has a temporal sense when applied to a terrestrial situation (for example, a 'perpetual' slave is a slave for the temporal duration of his life) it does not follow that the word need have exactly the same sense when applied to God: the subject must be allowed to qualify the meaning of the adjective. Barr insists that a philosophical and theological framework must be the context of any discussion of God's relation to time. Although word usage must be taken into account, simple appeal to lexical data is inconclusive, since it is too easy to read into the data the conclusions which we suppose we are reading out of them.[12]

But this leads us to a dilemma. We have already seen that the philosophical framework within which the Church formulated its

11. Cf. O. Cullmann *Christ and Time* pp. 45f.; Hermann Sasse *Theological Dictionary of the New Testatment* Vol. 1 pp. 197–209.
12. James Barr *Biblical Words for Time* pp. 68f, 158.

doctrines was heavily influenced by Platonism, and, this being the case, it was all but inevitable that the doctrine of eternity would be interpreted as timelessness. But we are now faced with the question as to whether that philosophical framework is adequate. And if we cannot turn to the biblical lexical data to evaluate the framework, since that would degenerate into question-begging, how *can* we evaluate it?

One thing we can do is to take a lesson from analytic philosophy and try to evaluate whether the concept of *vitae tota simul* is coherent: what would it mean to be in simultaneous possession of eternal life? This leads to the further question, prompted by our guiding motif of divine personhood, of whether, given our understanding of what it is for God to be personal, it is consistent to say that God could be timeless. Since the doctrine of divine personhood is fundamental, if it is incompatible with divine timelessness it is the latter which must be modified. I shall argue that this is indeed the case, and that this liberates us to discover a deeper understanding of the concept of divine eternity. And this, in turn, frees us to pursue a more holistic conception of the relationship between God and the world than would be possible if the doctrine of eternity had to be understood as timelessness. But this is to anticipate.

First, then, is the concept of a timeless living being coherent? We might begin with a more general question: do we have a concept of *any* timeless entity? Some candidates do present themselves: numbers, for instance, or universals, or certain sorts of truths like 'The hydrogen atom contains only one proton.'[13] It makes no sense to say of these, 'well, that may be true today, but did the hydrogen atom have only one proton yesterday?' or 'When did the number six begin?' There is, to be sure, philosophical controversy about the sense, if any, in which such truths, numbers and universals exist at all, but in whatever sense they can be said to exist, their existence is not what we might call historical. They do not begin or end; they do not change. But neither could they be properly described as omnitemporal, enduring throughout time. There is a sense, of course, in which the number six existed 'the same, yesterday, today, and for ever', but this is not because of its temporal longevity but because the number six is not the sort of thing to which time or temporal predicates properly apply. Thus in whatever sense entitites

13. The examples and much of the argument here are taken from William Kneale, 'Time and Eternity in Theology' pp. 94f.

46

like this might be said to exist, their existence could plausibly be said to be timeless.

But even if we grant this, could such entities serve as a model for divine timelessness? It may be that historically this is just what happened. Parmenides, in his reflections on the One, repudiated the possibility of using tensed language to describe it, and said that the One could not be the subject of any sort of temporal succession. In Plato, and even more in Plotinus, the One came increasingly to be identified with God. Sometimes Plotinus speaks of the One in mathematical terms, leading to a negative conception of the One involving timelessness and changelessness. But at other times the One is the giver of form and good and beauty, and is the Father and Maker, separate from what he makes.[14] When these two ways of thinking about the One are held together and given a Christian baptism, one result is a doctrine of divine eternity modelled on the timeless character of a mathematical entity.

Yet this raises many problems. It is difficult to see how the negative and positive characteristics of the One, held together in Plotinus's system by an appeal to mystical experience, could be translated into Christian theology without radical revisions. There are, after all, enormous differences between God and numbers, the most important of which is that the timeless quality of numbers is related to the fact that they are static. God, however, is the *living* God, the source of all life and the energy of all change. Could God still be coherently thought of as timeless in the way that static numbers are timeless, even though God is also in simultaneous possession of perfect eternal life?

Thomas Aquinas attempted to show that this would be possible. We can come to an understanding of the idea of divine eternity, he thought, by a two-step process. First, we realize that God's existence has no beginning and no end. This in itself, however, only gives us omnitemporality. The second step, therefore, is to recognize that, since God is immutable, there can be no before or after with God; all must be simultaneous for a changeless being. In this way we come to see that God's eternity is timelessness.[15] Unfortunately this does not get us very far. Leaving aside for the moment the problem about how a living being could be absolutely static, immutable, we still find that we have not after all been given any positive conception of timelessness. We have merely been told what it is *not* like –

14. A.H. Armstrong *The Architecture of the Intelligible Universe in the Philosophy of Plotinus* p. 14.
15. Thomas Aquinas *Summa Theologiae* I. Q.10. a.1.

it is not like time. But we knew this already, and it did not remove the puzzles.

A more interesting attempt to render the concept of divine time-lessness intelligible is made by Schleiermacher, whose efforts are all the more instructive for our purposes because he explicitly interprets God's relationship to space and time on parallel lines. Schleierma-cher's theological programme is to show how Christian doctrines arise out of and are rooted in the feeling of absolute dependence, which he believes to be the heart of true religion. In the case of divine eternity and incorporeality, the doctrines arise, he believes, because the feeling of absolute dependence requires that God is absolutely causal, or, to use the traditional theological term, omni-potent. Thus everything that happens in space and time is ultima-tely utterly dependent upon God. This means that there is an antithesis between the natural order and God, and it is this that generates the doctrine of divine eternity by contrast with the tempo-rality of the world. An exactly parallel argument is then used to show that God must also be utterly spaceless.[16]

Schleiermacher is well aware that a doctrine of divine timelessness cannot be allowed to denote a static God if it is to do justice to the personal and living nature of God. This is part of his point in setting the doctrine of eternity in the context of divine omnipotence or absolute causality, which, he emphasizes, is not a dead force, but the 'Absolute Vitality' of an omniscient (hence alive and conscious) God. Indeed, all of these attributes are really only different ways we have of expressing aspects of the same fact, the contrast between God and the world, and its absolute dependence upon him.

Schleiermacher next juxtaposes his parallel understanding of time and space with a doctrine of the omnipresence of God, another contour of our theological understanding. This, however, has a curious consequence. For if God is utterly timeless, contrasted with the whole temporal order, then one thing that God cannot be is the 'Eternal Now'. Some theologians have wanted to say this about God, but Schleiermacher recognizes that this is not a route open to him, because 'now' is a temporal term. To say that God's 'now' lasts for ever would presumably mean that God is omnitemporal, not timeless, and Schleiermacher vigorously rejects this. However, just as it follows that if God is utterly timeless he cannot be (tempo-rally) related to any time – not even 'now' – so also if God is utterly spaceless, he cannot be (spatially) related to any space – not even

16. Friedrich Schleiermacher *The Christian Faith* 51–3.

'here'. And if God cannot be *any*-where, confusion is increased, not resolved, by saying that God is *every*where – which is after all the literal meaning of omnipresence. Yet Schleiermacher seems oblivious to this.

When we explore these doctrines further in the context of Schleiermacher's theme of the feeling of absolute dependence, it is far from clear that he is right in giving them the meanings he does. He believes that his view of the relationship (or rather the lack of relationship) between God and time and space is derived from this religious consciousness: he says for instance that it is 'self-evident' that our feeling of absolute dependence implies a strong contrast between him on whom we depend and the causal structure of the spatio-temporal order. But is it self-evident? Surely on Schleiermacher's own terms, the religious consciousness, aware of its absolute dependence, is profoundly aware of God as 'here' and 'now', not as utterly unrelated to space and time. Of course, this 'here' cannot be interpreted as 'here and nowhere else', nor can 'now' mean 'now, but not yesterday or tomorrow': God is *omni*present in space and time. But this, given Schleiermacher's framework, would seem to lead rather to doctrines of omnitemporality and omnispatiality than to the idea of a timeless God who is nowhere. A very important aspect of the doctrines of divine eternity and omnipresence is their reminder that God cannot be limited to one particular location, temporally or spatially, but that his care extends infinitely beyond the boundaries of our own little individual worlds. But this greatness of God must not be taken to generate doctrines of divine timelessness and spacelessness, thus removing him altogether from our worlds, small as they may be: it can be better understood (as indeed popular religious consciousness does understand it) as implying that God is everywhere all the time. Clearly, some qualifications will be necessary in due course, but this seems a better initial position than an insistence on a sharp cleavage between God and the world.

Schleiermacher himself does try to preserve a very fundamental relationship between God and the world, in spite of his rejection of time and space as divine attributes. Indeed, the very way in which his notions of timelessness and spacelessness are generated is by thought about what is involved in causality, which is the dependence relationship between God and the world. This, however, does not help his case. If the world is causally dependent upon God in any meaningful sense, a temporal relationship is still required: creation and divine causal activity are *events* – that is, temporal. It is significant that Schleiermacher, in opting for a strong version of divine timelessness, was aware of this, at least with reference to the doctrine of creation: the old problem of whether God existed before the creation of the world again raises its head. Consequently Schleiermacher argues that God's relationship to the universe should be thought of as one of eternal preservation; this is his demythologized version of the doctrine of *creatio ex nihilo*.

Unfortunately, however, the doctrine of preservation cannot escape temporal implications any more than can the doctrine of creation. It is true that a doctrine of preservation avoids the need to postulate a temporal beginning. Still, preservation means that things are *kept*, they are sustained in being over time. Thus any relation of causality interpreted as preservation requires that the preserver is involved in a temporal relationship with that which he preserves, so that it continues to exist. But the notion of continuity is as temporal a notion as is that of beginning or end. Even if creation could be reinterpreted as preservation, therefore, preservation itself could not dispense with the temporal notion of continuity.

Furthermore, it is hard to see how we could manage theologically without any doctrine of creation, at least in its broader sense. Perhaps we need not insist that God created the universe out of nothing at some point in time; we will reconsider this later. But we can hardly dispense with all notions of divine creativity: his action in the world, bringing order out of chaos, and developing his purposes by providence or miracle. Yet none of this would be possible for a timeless being.[17] Thus the notion of timelessness is an inappropriate one for the living God of Christian theology; it would at best find application to such abstract and static entities as numbers and universals. Life involves change – succession – and if that life is causally related to the world, the causality as much as the life itself demands the applicability of temporal predicates.

This, however, has further implications, for it means that the doctrine of immutability is not one with which Christian theology can be content. Of course Christian theologians do set great store by the changelessness of God: this is the basis of our trust in his loving intentions towards us – we need not fear that tomorrow God will be different and will treat us differently, like some whimsical despot. But we can make a distinction between this changelessness of character, without which we would not have a basis for trust in God, and the absolute changelessness entailed by a doctrine of divine timelessness. It has been pointed out many times that these

17. Nelson Pike *God and Timelessness* pp. 110f.

are not equivalent: a person with an unchanging character and purpose may change his methods to fit varying contingencies as they arise, may respond to requests and attitudes, and have real relations with other persons and things, whereas an absolutely immutable being could do none of these things. Yet even granting this distinction, it remains true that many theologians have insisted, with Augustine, that God is *absolutely* immutable; this indeed was the basis from which they welcomed the doctrine of timelessness.

It is most significant for our purposes how this was also linked with the doctrine of divine incorporeality. Time is necessary for change, and without time there can be no change. And in closely parallel thought, matter is that which undergoes the changes: in the Aristotelian tradition taken up by Thomas Aquinas, matter is the pure potentiality for change. Thus since God is timeless, he must be changeless, and since he has no potentiality for change, he must be immaterial. But the connections can equally well be stated in reverse order. An incorporeal God is by definition immune from the very possibility of change, because only matter is mutable. But time and change hang together; thus an immutable God is a timeless God. Both timelessness and incorporeality exclude even the bare logical possibility of change. It would be mistaken to select any of these concepts as the conclusion and the others as the premises; they do not constitute an argument so much as a cluster of interrelated notions, any of which evoke the others.

The Thomistic term for God as self-subsistent Being, immune from the possibility of change, is 'pure act', and forms the complete contrast to matter, which is 'pure potentiality'. In a well-known passage, Thomas contrasts God and matter like this:

> . . . In the First Existent thing everything must be actual; there can be no potentiality whatsoever. For although, when we consider things coming to exist, potential existence precedes actual existence in these particular things; nevertheless, absolutely speaking, actual existence takes precedence of potential existence. For what is able to exist is brought into existence only by what already exists. Now we have seen that the first existent is God. In God then there can be no potentiality. In bodies, however, there is always potentiality, for the external as such is always potential of division. God, therefore, cannot have a body.[18]

When Thomas Aquinas says that God is the First Existent, he is

18. Thomas Aquinas *Summa Theologiae* I.a.3.1.

not in conflict with the doctrine of divine timelessness in the sense of saying that God is temporally first. Instead, saying that God is the First Cause means for Aquinas what speaking of God as Absolute Causality means for Schleiermacher: the universe and everything in it is contingent, utterly dependent upon God. If God did not exist, nothing else would, and if God could somehow suddenly cease to exist, the universe could not continue to exist without him. Thus the universe as it actually is, with all its built-in potentialities, exists only because God actually exists: Aquinas holds that this would be true even if the universe is without beginning.

But might we not suggest that, while the existence of the universe requires the actual existence of God, it leaves open the possibility that God is also in some respects potential, and thus perhaps temporal and in some ways mutable? Clearly God could not be *pure* potentiality – utter changeableness – and be First Cause, but why must he be *pure* act? Could he not (like any other existing thing) be a mixture? Thomas would find this impossible. God is, in the first place, utterly simple, which no mixture could ever be. Furthermore, God is perfect, and a perfect being could not be in potentiality because it is by definition complete. All of this is involved in the assertion that God is, without qualification, First Cause.

We can see more clearly what Thomas meant if we ask how, if there were potentiality in God, it could ever be actualized. Only two answers are possible: it could be actualized by the universe (or some part of it), or else direct self-actualization could take place. The former would mean that the universe, or the relevant part of it, had the power – the potential – to affect God. But since Aquinas believed that God is the First Cause, he held that the universe and all its potential is ultimately derived from God in the first place; thus if the universe could somehow actualize God, this would still be only an indirect form of self-actualization. But then if all possible actualization of divine potentiality would have to come from God anyway, directly or indirectly, what sense can it make to speak of real potentiality in God? As Aquinas has already argued, only that which is in actuality can change something potential to something actual – for example, only application of actual heat can make potentially hot water actually hot. If God would already have to be actual in respect x to actualize his potential in respect x, then surely it is absurd to suppose that he is really potential in respect x at all. The whole exercise is pointless. If God is really First Cause in the full sense of the term, he must be pure act, in no way potential, hence immutable, hence incorporeal, and hence timeless.

But this argument is not watertight; furthermore, if it were accepted, it would rule out the possibility of a religiously adequate theology. The premise that nothing can be changed from potentiality to actuality except by something already actual is far from true. It might have passed unquestioned, especially when we are given the example of fire having to be hot to make the kettle boil, because when we think in terms of inanimate objects this seems like common sense. But it is worth reflecting that inanimate objects are the things, on any account, *least* like God in the whole created universe, and are therefore presumably poor sources for analogies. As soon as we think instead about persons and their potentialities, the axiomatic premise begins to look very dubious. Suppose young Mozart has the potential to become a great musician, indeed, to write the G minor Symphony. Surely we must not suppose that this symphony is already actual in order for his potential to write it to be actualized. It will not do to say that Mozart is the actual entity which makes the potential symphony actual, because what we want to know is how the potential *in Mozart* is actualized; how does he get from being a potential composer to being its actual composer? No doubt there are debts to things actual: his parents, his teachers, previous musical compositions. But unless we deny that there is any such thing as creativity, the list of debts cannot tell the *whole* story; there is genuinely new actualization of a potential. In fact, the original premise, although making sense as an antidote to theories of spontaneous generation or occurrences without sufficient cause in the physical world, is wholly inappropriate to personal agents and their creativity. When we come to works of art, or indeed to any creativity of thought or action, there is no reason to suppose that there can be nothing new under the sun, and that all depends on antecedently existing actuality.

Someone might object, however, that this misses the point about God being the First Cause. All things utterly depend upon him, and so although of course Mozart's symphony was not actual *under* the sun before he wrote it, he could only write it because his potentiality to do so was actualized by God: God cannot be encountered by novelty, even though we can be. Even if there is creative change at a human level, this is not analogous to the divine level; for God, as the source of all change, must himself be unchanging.

Such an objection, though, would be misguided. In the first place, it raises enormous questions about the possibility of genuine human freedom and creativity: if all is already somehow actual in God, including our choices and their results, then a doctrine of strict predestination could hardly be avoided. Whatever is true in the statement that God is in some sense the source and goal of all, it can hardly mean this. But furthermore, if God were immutable in this strict sense, then not only is real creativity impossible for us, it is impossible even for God himself. If God is immutable, then it is impossible for him ever to act in any way: he cannot think, cannot respond affectively or actively to the affairs of the world, cannot in any sense be a causal agent (as opposed to, say, a magnetic force, drawing the world towards itself without intentionality, like Aristotle's Unmoved Mover) because all of these are events, involving time and change. God could not reveal himself, could not work a miracle, and could not become incarnate or manifest himself in a human being. Indeed, God could not have made the world or be creatively involved in its development. To be creative is to bring about something new, and this involves change in its most basic sense in the creator too, not just in the thing that is being created. But if God were pure act, without any potentiality, then he would be incapable of doing anything whatever – yet creativity is the first attribute of God mentioned in Scripture, and its emphasis throughout is on his responsive activity.

Anselm wrestled with this problem long ago: how could he square God's timelessness and immutability, which he accepted, with God's responsiveness and power? He believes that when we are distressed, we can experience the compassion and consolation of God. Yet if God is compassionate, does this not mean that he feels a sympathetic response? And if he does, surely this is at variance with his immutability. Anselm resolves his problem by an appeal to the distinction between external and internal relations: the compassion of God is *our* experience, not God's; and although it makes a difference to the way we relate to God, it makes no difference in God himself – thus God remains utterly changeless. Anselm says:

> Truly, thou art so in terms of our experience, but thou art not so in terms of thine own. For, when thou beholdest us in our wretchedness, we experience the effect of compassion, but thou dost not experience the feeling ... Thou art affected by no sympathy for wretchedness.[19]

By extension, anything which we might call God's action in the universe would have to be explained in the same way: the newness, the change, is only in the world, not in God.

19. Anselm *Proslogion* VIII.

But few religious believers will be satisfied with this response. In the first place, it would mean that God could not think or perceive or have any conscious processes, because these would involve changes in God. Sometimes theologians have tried to circumvent this by appeal to the doctrine of omniscience, interpreting it to mean that God does not think, he *knows*, timelessly and immutably. This however has the result that any genuinely free choice of a human being, which, if it is truly free, could not be known in advance, could never, even after its occurrence, be known by God, because this would imply a change in God. In addition, it would mean that God could never do and could never have done anything at all, because any activity is a change from having the potentiality to do an act to having actually done it. It is impossible consistently to attribute to God both creative activity and the doctrine that he is pure act. Far from being omnipotent, a God who is pure act cannot do anything at all.

It is true, of course, that willing a change is not the same as changing the will; and it has sometimes been argued that God could have eternally and changelessly willed that certain events happen at specified times. Thus Richard Swinburne suggests that we might be able to preserve a doctrine of changelessness by attributing all actions to God's fixed intentions which he has had 'from all eternity', with the intentions varying according to the outcome of contingent human actions.[20] But in the end even this cannot save the day for a doctrine of divine immutability, as we can see if we ask what makes one of the contingency plans become operational. Surely it is not just God's intention, but his activity: God not only wills, which perhaps he could do from all eternity if it makes sense to speak of a timeless will; he also *brings about* what he wills, and this involves creative relationship with events occurring in the temporal order.

Nor is it simply a frailty of our nature but part of the meaning of the word 'event' that events are temporal. Even for God, it is impossible, as we have seen, that events should be timeless. God may well experience time differently from the way we do; we will explore this possibility below. But that does not mean that for him everything could be simultaneous rather than successive, let alone that he is not related to time at all. Creation, action and suffering are events, not just in our psychological structures, but as part of the meaning of the terms.

20. Richard Swinburne *The Coherence of Theism* p. 214.

The point of departure for our understanding of God has been that he is personal, and that his personal nature must be taken as central to theology in such a way that, in any case of conflict, the conflict must be resolved in a way which heightens, rather than diminishes, our understanding of his personal nature. Yet a God who is pure act, with no potentiality to create or think, to perceive or act or love, is a God who may have some affinities with Aristotle's Unmoved Mover, but who seems further and further removed from a biblical concept of a living God who loves and cares, and is powerful to act and even to give himself on behalf of the downtrodden and oppressed. If Jesus of Nazareth was in any sense revelatory of the nature of God, that nature can hardly have been what Aristotle thought it was.

Philosophers like Pike and Swinburne who are in sympathy with this conclusion think that it is theologically unproblematical. Their view is that we can substitute a doctrine of everlastingness, which will do all the duties of a doctrine of eternity without generating the problems raised by timelessness. But will it? The Fathers and subsequent theologians who have insisted on divine timelessness were after all not blind to the problems which such a notion raises; furthermore they were well aware of the alternative of everlastingness and firmly rejected it. Why? It is not good enough to say that they were wedded to Platonism: they could liberate themselves from that marriage when it became inconvenient, as we can see from their stance on the doctrine of creation *ex nihilo*. It would be worth looking again, therefore, at their adoption of the doctrine of timelessness to see whether we are not after all sacrificing something of religious importance which everlastingness cannot replace.

The first clue comes from Augustine, who as we saw, tried to resolve his problems by saying that time itself was created by God. Now if what I have said so far is correct, then this is a hopeless muddle: time is not a 'thing', and to speak of it as being created requires illegitimate reification; furthermore creation itself is an event and thus is temporal. But even if we reject Augustine's solution, it is still worth probing more deeply into his thoughts: the *Confessions* is after all primarily a spiritual treatise, and the philosophical speculations are subservient to that purpose. From the context it becomes clear that Augustine is trying to retain a strong view of God's sovereignty: God is subject to nothing, but all things are subject to him. If Augustine could say that God is the *maker* of time, then it would follow that God is the *master* of time;

time has no dominion over him. And this would be a conclusion which Augustine could hardly help but welcome.

But what would such sovereignty over time amount to? Obviously it means, in the first place, that God is not subject to age, senility and death, nor, on the other end of the scale, to birth and infancy. This in itself, however, could also be preserved by a doctrine of divine everlastingness: it is inappropriate to ask whether God is middle-aged or old, since terms like these presuppose a scale of measurement, an 'average' life-span against which an individual can be compared. If God is everlasting, he is without beginning and end, and therefore without age. In that sense, he is not subject to time.

There is, however, a pathos about our subjection to time which would not disappear even if we could drink from the fountain of eternal youth, and that is what we might call the fleetingness of our experiences. Even if we could live for ever, the most treasured moments of our lives pass away and are gone from us for ever. Not even the most vivid memory is the same as the event, and although we invest in cameras and photograph albums to try to 'capture the moment', we all know that looking at old photographs can at best conjure up memories and nostalgia for the life that then was, it cannot bring that life back. But it seems inappropriate to attribute that same fleetingness to God, even if we couple it with a completely accurate divine memory. God must be sovereign over the sort of change and chance which we experience as the fleetingness of time, and a doctrine of divine everlastingness seems hard-pressed to account for this.

Another part of the same issue is that what we experience as the swift passage of time carries with it not only irrevocable loss of the past but also the ambiguities of the present and the uncertainties of the future. Time will not stand still, even when we are faced with a moral decision of enormous consequences; often we are unable to postpone action until all the data have been duly considered, and must simply do the best we can in an ambiguous situation. It was this which caused Karl Barth to say, in his *Römerbrief*, that faith involves recognition of 'the qualitative distinction between time and eternity':[21] God's eternity makes him sovereign over the uncertainties with which we are forced to contend.

If we press these religious considerations into a philosophical mould, what comes out is a series of difficulties with the doctrine

21. Karl Barth *Römerbrief* 1922 Edition, p. 10.

of omniscience. As we have seen, the notion of timelessness is nowadays often abandoned in favour of everlastingness partly because knowledge of temporal events is incompatible with timelessness; it therefore comes as something of a surprise to find that part of the reason earlier theologians insisted on timelessness was that they felt that only a timeless God *could* be omniscient. This is quite clear in Boethius's discussion, where he says that God's eternity understood as simultaneous possession of eternal life is the very thing that makes it possible for God to know the past and the future with an immediacy which would be ruled out by attributing to him merely an acute memory and a particularly sharp ability for prediction. For Boethius, that would not be good enough. Divine knowledge, he believed, must be immediate, not mediated by anything – not even memory or forecast. Putting it another way, he could not allow that God could lose his past the way we – even if we had good memories – do lose it. It does not help to appeal at this point back to the doctrine of omniscience, for if omniscience is to be compatible with everlastingness, it will have to be reinterpreted along the lines of memory and prediction rather than immediate knowledge and we are right back to the beginning again.

So we are left with a dilemma: omniscience cannot be squared with timelessness, because a timeless God could not know or respond to temporal events. But it also cannot be squared with everlastingness because this would undermine claims to the immediacy of divine knowledge, making God dependent on memory and prediction, and subject to the fleetingness of time.

Although he does not address himself to this problem in precisely these terms, Karl Barth wrestles valiantly with this dilemma. On first reading, his account seems hopelessly incoherent. On the one hand he repudiates simple everlastingness:

> Eternity is not . . . an infinite extension of time both backwards and forwards. Time can have nothing to do with God. The infinity of its own extension cannot help it. For even and especially in this extension there is the separation and distance and contradiction which mark it as time and distinguish it from eternity as the creature from the Creator.[22]

On the other hand, Barth rejects a sharp contrast between time and eternity, and characterizes divine eternity by what must be regarded as temporal predicates. God, he says, is pre-temporal,

22. Karl Barth *Church Dogmatics* II.1. p.608.

supra-temporal and post-temporal. He is absolutely sovereign over time, and in no way subject to its fleetingness; yet Barth also says that:

God's eternity is itself beginning, succession and end . . . God is both the prototype and foreordination of all being, and therefore also the prototype and foreordination of time. God has time because and as he has eternity.[23]

Furthermore, Barth says that the Christian message itself

depends on the fact that God was and is and is to be, that our existence stands under the sign of a divine past, present and future . . . Without God's complete temporality the content of the Christian message has no shape.[24]

Barth concedes that this makes God's time and eternity 'a complete mystery', but adds that it is also 'completely simple' – all we need do is to contemplate and adore God in his triune nature and we will know eternity, for this is God's essence.

Now as it stands, this seems to me to be nonsense – but edifying nonsense nonetheless. The edification does not arise from Barth's admonition to adore we know not what, however, but rather from his refusal to sacrifice what he feels crucial on both sides of the debate: God's sovereignty over time as well as God's temporal involvement with the world. But is there any way in which these two could be reconciled?

We might begin by reviewing a well-known distinction, namely that between the objective passage of time and our subjective awareness of it. The subjective experience is expressed in some lines by Pentreath:

For when I was a babe and wept and slept,
    Time crept;
When I was a boy and laughed and talked,
    Time walked;
Then when the years saw me a man,
    Time ran;
But as I older grew,
    Time flew.

We do not need to make any alterations in our notion of objective

23. Ibid. p. 611.
24. Ibid. p. 620.

59

time, time as measured by clocks, to see the point of these words: the planets revolve around the sun and the earth rotates at just the same rate on a rainy day when time drags as on a day filled with too much activity for its hours; still, we experience it differently.

Of particular interest in connection with our subjective experience of time is what we experience as the present. Henri Bergson, in his book *Time and Free Will*, discussed our consciousness of the present as duration. When we have an experience like listening to a piece of music or being told a joke, the completion of the experience depends on our ability to hold the whole of it together as a unit. But he points out that our consciousness, when thus engaged, does not take the individual sounds as a bare succession, like a series of points in a line, but makes the whole into an organic unity. Bergson uses this as a springboard for his idealist analysis of objective time, which I do not propose to investigate further. But his comments about the way in which the distinctness and yet the unity of items of our consciousness are experienced merit reflection. I listen to a piece of music, and if it pauses on the leading note I feel suspended until it resolves into the tonic: the phrase forms a unit for consciousness. But clearly this does not mean that it is all simultaneous: that would be noise, not a musical phrase. This comes out even more clearly if we take the example of a clock striking. If there were no experience of successive strikes we should have no alternative to saying that it struck only once; yet these very successive strikes are held together until they cease and we can say what time it is.

William James made a study of this sort of subjective awareness in his *Principles of Psychology*. He argued that our apprehension of what we call the present is in reality a unit of the recent past which is held together in our consciousness: obvious examples are musical phrases, or series of words joined to form sentences. His assumption is that the present is a durationless instant, so that if we are immediately conscious of a succession as in the striking of a clock we cannot without contradiction call the whole time of the successive strikes the real present but only its latest boundary. Yet to our consciousness the whole series is immediate in a way which is different from what we would normally call memory. Thus to differentiate it both from the real present and from the past, it is referred to as the specious present.[25]

The idea of a specious present has been attacked from different directions. On one side are those like C.W.K. Mundle who object

25. William James *Principles of Psychology* Vol. I p. 609f.

to the assumption that the present is a durationless instant. Mundle argues that our view of what the *real* present is would differ depending on whether we held to a representative or a phenomenalist theory of perception: if we held to the latter, we need not define the present as a durationless instant, and hence what James and others refer to as the *specious* present could more properly be called the *conscious* present, in which temporal relations can be sense-given. On the other side are those like J.D. Mabbott who object to the suggestion that experiences like the striking of a clock which must by definition be comprised of successive elements should be called present: part of the experience is *not* present, but immediately past, and our consciousness of this part is properly called memory, albeit of a very special sort.[26]

To take sides in this dispute would lead us far away from the present task. Fortunately for our purposes we do not need to do so, because all sides agree that our subjective experience of musical phrases, jokes, striking clocks, and the like does differ both from other sorts of memory and from what might be called instantaneous experiences. So whether we call it a special sort of memory or an awareness of the contents of a special sort of 'present', the main point is that we do have subjective experiences which somehow hold together in a unity that which is objectively successive. I shall in what follows use the term 'specious present', though nothing that I have to say hangs on this usage.

More germane to our project is the question of how long the specious present lasts. William James thought that it varied from a few seconds to a minute; his opinion was based on experiments by Wundt which tested the ability of subjects to retain and identify groups of sounds. As Mabbott points out, however, this experiment might be more appropriately seen as a test of memory than as a way of determining the unit of temporal experience; furthermore, this could at best produce the unit of temporal experience for *hearing* – the other senses might be quite different. Probably what is experienced as a conscious whole, a specious present, varies between individuals and between sorts of experience. Most of us perceive polysyllabic words as wholes, probably sentences, and perhaps groups of sentences, as in jokes or philosophical arguments. There is a famous story about Mozart according to which he once claimed

26. C.W.K. Mundle 'Time, Consciousness of' in Paul Edwards, ed. *The Encyclopedia of Philosophy* Vol. 8 pp. 134–8. Cf. Mundle's 'How Specious is the Specious Present?' in *Mind* Vol. LXIII (1954) pp. 26–48. For the opposite view, see J.D. Mabbott 'Our Direct Experience of Time' in *Mind* Vol. LX (1951) pp. 153–67.

to experience an entire musical composition as a whole before he wrote it down. And mystics are wont to say that in their most intense encounters with God time stops, not in the sense that there is no succession, but in the sense that the succession is somehow experienced holistically. In the light of the preceding considerations, their claims may not be quite such dark sayings as they at first seem to be. There is after all no *a priori* reason why the specious present should not be longer in some sorts of experience than in others, especially if they are very intense.

But the point to which all this is leading is that, if we can apply this to God, we may be able to retain at least some of the important ingredients of interpreting eternity as timelessness without lapsing into the incoherencies we have already discovered. The problem, after all, was that God cannot be timeless in the objective sense; that is, he must be aware of events and must be able to respond. But from this nothing follows about God's subjective experience. Now suppose we take our subjective experience of certain sorts of events and apply it to God. Taking into account the doctrine of omniscience, which implies that all God's mental contents must be immediately present to him and in this sense no distinction can be made between divine knowledge and divine memory, it would appear that in God's case the specious present could be of much greater duration than in ours – in fact, everlasting. All the past must be immediately present to God's consciousness. But this does *not* mean that all is simultaneous, that there can be no succession. Just as our experience of a musical phrase, though we experience it as a whole, requires that, objectively speaking, there is a succession of sounds rather than that all the notes are heard simultaneously, so also the attribution of an everlasting specious present to God does not mean that he is timeless in the objective sense, but the very opposite.

If this is correct, then God could be aware of the temporal succession of events and could respond to them in a personal way, on analogy with our awareness and response to the succession in a piece of music. Yet on the other hand he need not be subject to what I have called the fleetingness of experience. All of the past could be held together in the divine consciousness; it need never be lost to God as it is to us. This is not just a reversion to acute divine memory, for as we have seen in our own case, there is a distinction between ordinary memory and our perception of the objectively earlier elements of a particular specious present: the first notes of a musical phrase are not remembered as ordinary past events but are taken up into our experience of the whole of the phrase, to become a unity without losing the objectively successive character. A further attraction of this suggestion is that it makes it possible for us to see how the past could be immediately present to God, without having to say that God could change the past. If we said, in the old sense, that God is literally timeless, then it would seem that, if God could act at all, he could act equally in the past as in the present, since it would not, to him, *be* past. But this is absurd. Not even Boethius, expounding on divine eternity in prison, would pray that God would bring it about that the Senate had not condemned him some months previously. The presence of the past to God, we might say, is necessary for the doctrine of omniscience, impossible for the doctrine of omnipotence. The puzzle is resolved if we apply a notion of specious present to God, for then the past can be a part of the immediate contents of divine consciousness without any implications about the ability of God to change or act upon that past, any more than we can alter the first words of a sentence we utter when we are coming to the end of it.

The idea of a divine specious present gains both clarity and plausibility when we see how its application illuminates some of Karl Barth's comments which are otherwise enigmatic. I am not suggesting that Barth himself had this in mind; but he struggled to retain what he felt to be religiously important, even when this resulted in 'mystery'. We have seen that Barth rejected the reinterpretation of eternity as everlastingness; yet he also says, commenting on the incarnation:

> The God who does this and therefore can do it is obviously in himself both timeless and temporal. He is timeless in that the defects of our time, its fleetingness and its separations, are alien to him and disappear, and in him all beginning, continuation and ending form a unique Now, steadfast yet moving, moving yet steadfast.[27]

If this is taken to refer to objective time it is an exercise in self-contradiction which no amount of piety can dissipate. But if we took Barth here as drawing a distinction between God's objective temporality demonstrated in his activity in history through Jesus of Nazareth and his subjective experience in which all is held together in a 'moving yet steadfast' unique Now, this otherwise opaque saying might be illuminated.

27. Karl Barth *Church Dogmatics* II.1.p.617.

In fact, this distinction can be used to make sense of much of Barth's discussion of divine eternity which without it makes nonsense. For although he says that 'time can have nothing to do with God' he also says that time is included in God's duration; time is presupposed in eternity, which negates only its problematical aspects and its fleetingness. If we take eternity as the name for God's all-inclusive specious present, then we can see both its contrast from ordinary temporal succession – the *simul* of eternity – and also how time is presupposed in it. Thus objectively God is everlasting, but his subjective experience is eternal. Barth says:

> As the eternal One who as such has and himself is absolutely real time, he gives us the relatively but in this way genuinely real time proper to us. As the eternal One he is present personally at every point of our time. As the eternal One it is he who surrounds our time and rules it with all that it contains. How can he be and do all this if as the eternal One he does not himself have his own time, superior to ours, undisturbed by the fleetingness and separations of our time, simultaneous with all our times but in this way and for this reason absolutely real time?[28]

Barth himself would not be happy with this attempt to draw a distinction between objective time and internal time consciousness. Nevertheless if he did accept it, it would help him to retain some of the things he considers indispensable without collapsing into obscurity.

Significantly, the same can be said of other writers who wrestle with the concept of eternity: if we look, for example, at the accounts of Thomas Aquinas or Anselm with this distinction in mind, it is striking in its results. I do not have space to substantiate this in detail, and will look briefly at only one example, that of Boethius. His definition of eternity gave impetus, as we saw, to the idea that God is timeless, with its attendant problems. But what if we took this to apply, not to God's relation to objective time, which would be better described as everlastingness, but to God's subjective experience of temporal events: the whole, perfect, simultaneous possession of endless life. Since in the context Boethius is concerned to give an account of divine knowledge, this has some initial plausibility. The doctrine of eternity interpreted as simultaneity is the key, for him, to the divine nature which makes omniscience possible. Now if this is taken not as timelessness in the objective sense but as

28. Ibid.

an infinitely extended specious present, we can preserve Boethius's common sense about the unalterability of the past and still make sense of a comment like this one:

> Since, then, every judgement comprehends the subjects presented to it according to its own nature, and since God lives in the eternal present, his *knowledge* transcends all movement of time and abides in the simplicity of its immediate present. It . . . regards all things in its simple comprehension as if they were now taking place.[29]

But there are problems. Anyone familiar with Barth or Boethius will have noticed that in quoting from them I have omitted reference to God's knowledge of the future – yet they would both insist that part of the point of the doctrine of eternity was to elucidate how God can have foreknowledge. Now even if my suggestion about God's knowledge of the past and present makes sense, could the specious present be extended to what is objectively future?

There is one consideration which might lead us a short way towards assent, and that is the experience known as *déjà vu* – the feeling that we get in some situations that we have been through all this before and know in advance exactly what will happen. Might we expand this notion of *déjà vu* in God's case as the future part of the specious present, and thus try to account for divine foreknowledge? I think the answer must be negative; because following this line of thought soon leads one into making absurd claims. In the specious present, we take up experiences which are objectively past into a whole with those which are still occurring: because the former are objectively past, it makes no sense to speak of changing them. Now if our – or God's – experience of the future were to be interpreted along parallel lines to this experience of the past – if God 'remembered' the future – then the events of the future must be as unchangeable as the past. It is not just difficult, it is logically impossible to change the past; and if the future is really *just* like the past to God then it too is absolutely rigid. Enough has been written about the difficulties of foreknowledge interpreted in this strong sense to make it unnecessary for me to go into detail.[30]

Still, this need not bring us quite to a full stop. William James, when he first discussed the idea of the specious present, said: 'The present is a saddleback on which we sit perched and from which

29. Boethius *Consolation of Philosophy* V.6, emphasis mine.
30. Cf. Anthony Kenny *The God of the Philosophers*.

we look in two directions in time.'[31] He meant, I think, that we are directly aware of the immediate future in the same way as we are directly aware of the immediate past, and intended the term 'specious present' to cover both. As I have said, I do not think this makes sense; I do not think we can be *directly* aware of any future event, and that that is a matter of the logic of 'future' not a frailty of our perception. And if that is correct, then it is correct also for God. But James could be interpreted in a weaker sense. From our present position we do, of course, *predict* the future, sometimes with considerable accuracy. Furthermore these predictions affect our experience of the present: if we could predict with reasonable confidence that we would die tonight we would experience the remaining hours of the day with much greater intensity.

Now it would make considerable sense to say that God (logically) could not know the future *as* he knows the past, but that he can make absolutely accurate and complete predictions about it; and these predictions are incorporated into and modify his experience of the specious present to a correspondingly greater extent than they do in the case of our finite experience. Boethius and Barth would hardly be content with this as an account of the presence of the future to God, but I see no way in which they could consistently have more. And this view does, at least, seem to provide *some* of the positive aspects of what has traditionally been included in the doctrine of divine eternity. Not only does God live for ever, but his life and experience is not hampered in the way that ours is by the passage of time; he experiences it holistically rather than in our fragmented way. Perhaps after all this is only another way of saying that God is omniscient: present, past and future are all objectively real enough, but all are open to his immediate knowledge; the past does not recede from his memory and the future is not unforeseen. And through it all he remains, not immutable, but constant in his character of loving and merciful God, a God who is alive and conscious and active, not impersonal and static.

31. James op.cit. p. 609.

5

Personhood and Embodiment

'People are what you meet.'[1] With this slogan, Antony Flew points to the difficulties involved in trying to conceptualize disembodied persons. All our language about persons and their activities, ourselves included, is developed in a context where people can be met – that is, a context of embodied persons. And this is the very language which theists wish to apply to a personal God. This raises an acute problem for traditional Christian theology. On the one hand, a theism which can be called Christian must affirm that God is personal; yet orthodoxy has also said that God is incorporeal: could an incorporeal God really have *personal* characteristics and abilities?

In the previous chapter, we saw that traditional theism has held to a doctrine of divine timelessness. However, when we disentangled the threads of that notion, we could retain what is religiously important in the doctrine of eternity without having to accept doctrines of immutability and pure act that would jeopardize the personal nature of God, turning him into an unresponsive and uncreative Unmoved Mover. In this and subsequent chapters, I wish to move along similar lines in a discussion of the notion of space. By untying the knots in the doctrines of God's relationship to matter we are liberated, I shall suggest, to deepen our understanding of the personal nature of God's power, knowledge and presence without abandoning those features of the doctrine of incorporeality which are religiously important. To do this we will use once again our model of embodied human personhood, qualifying it when (but not before) it becomes necessary to do so in our efforts to apply it to a personal God.

A strong pull towards the rejection of the possibility of disembodied personhood at a human level comes from a major philosophical objection to dualism, the theory that consciousness is brain-dependent. This theory can take various forms; we need not survey

1. A.G.N. Flew 'Some Objections to Cartesian Views of Man' p. 26.

them here. The important common denominator is that memory, consciousness, dispositions, thoughts – all are rooted in the brain and central nervous system. In strong forms of central state materialism, this premise is made the basis of outright denial of the existence of mental phenomena; but a milder interpretation is possible, in which mental phenomena are reinterpreted as the functions of the central nervous system 'felt from the inside', so to speak. In this form of the identity theory, two sorts of language are often felt to be necessary, language having 'mental' terms, and language having 'physical' terms, to account for the 'inside' and the 'outside' of a single physical reality. But what is important for all the versions of this theory is that if the physical reality were destroyed – if there were irreversible disintegration of the brain and central nervous system – then there could no longer be consciousness, thought, or memory. If the brain is destroyed, so is the self.

There is considerable pressure from common sense to accept some such position. We are quite aware of how tiredness or drugs affect our mental ability, and of how concussion or more severe brain damage can make consciousness impossible. From this point of view it is counter-intuitive to suppose that, although in our experience mental activities are consistently impaired proportionally to brain damage, complete *cessation* of functioning of the brain and central nervous system would somehow be the signal for mental rejuvenation instead of utter collapse, so that we would thereby attain to life more fully conscious than we have ever before experienced, 'knowing as we are known' in a disembodied state. Our intuitions may be mistaken, of course. But in view of the counter-intuitiveness of such newness of life, and since our daily experience of persons is an experience without exception of embodied persons, the onus rests on the upholder of incorporeal personhood to explain what he means and how he thinks it possible.

This will not be an easy task. Edgar Wilson, reviewing the empirical data in an argument for a modified identity theory, says:

There is considerable circumstantial evidence from comparative anatomy and psychology correlating both phylogenetic and onto-genetic development of brain size and complexity with corresponding developments in manifest intelligence. This strongly suggests that brain structure is a necessary condition . . . for mind.[2]

If this is correct, then disembodied survival is impossible. We have

2. Edgar Wilson *The Mental as Physical* p. 56.

already seen that a dualist picture of a person as a mind and a body which could come apart at death is not a picture which Christian anthropology need retain; so it might be thought that a theist need not feel threatened by statements like this one. However, if one agrees with Wilson that mental activities are a function of physical activities of the brain and central nervous system in such a strong sense that the brain is *necessary* for mind, then a theistic position is called into question. If brain is indispensable for mental activities, then either God has a brain, or else God has no mental activities – but the latter is equivalent to saying that traditional theism, and any postulation of a personal God, is false.

Now, I wish to argue in subsequent sections that it is advantageous philosophically and religiously to view the universe as God's body rather than thinking of God and the world as utterly separated into a cosmic dualism. But this will hardly mean that some part of the universe is God's brain! To speak of the universe as God's body will involve some new ways of thinking about the world, and some of these may appear startling: we will investigate as we proceed what this involves and also what it does not involve. It is important to see that certain sorts of qualifications are immediately necessary, and that these qualifications eliminate from the beginning some spontaneous adverse reactions which would otherwise be natural, while at the same time raising some further problems. For example, it might be thought that to suggest that the universe is to God as our bodies are to us implies that the universe must be a set of 'divine organs' – a preposterous notion. It would be presumptuous to try to say how the universe is organized in terms of divine function, let alone think that it had to be organized like our own bodies. By listing a few speculations we get a feel for how silly they are: this galaxy is God's liver, those nebulae are his eyes, perhaps his brain is a black hole? Obviously this is as senseless as it is religiously repulsive: whatever we mean by suggesting that the universe is God's body, this cannot be a part of it. Yet rejection of such absurdity leaves us still with the problem: if brain is necessary for mind, then would we not have to say that if God exists, something in the universe is God's brain?

But this is not only foolish theology, it is bad philosophy as well. Why should we say that brain is a necessary condition for mind – let alone brain as organized in *Homo sapiens*? Even if we accept an identity theory and agree that in all of our experiences mental events are either a product of brain events or another way of describing them, this is still nothing more than an empirical generalization. It does not follow that brain is *necessary* for mind: conceivably there are things without brains which nevertheless are (or could become) conscious. Would we be prepared, for instance, to rule out *a priori* the possibility of developing robots which acquired consciousness? Or to say that if there is conscious life on other planets it *must* be of the same organic structure as our own? Unless we have *defined* mental activity as activity dependent upon a brain of specific construction, there seems no possible way that we could know in advance that things made of very different hard- or soft-ware from ourselves could not have consciousness and other mental abilities. Thus Wilson's suggestion that brain is a necessary condition of mind is much too strong. No empirical evidence could ever prove it, and making it true by stipulation would be out of order: it would, for instance, decide the question of the mental ability of extra-terrestrial beings which might be discovered in future exploration of outer space solely on the grounds of organic structure, irrespective of their ability to communicate with us, remember, calculate, and do other such things which we normally classify as 'mental'. Nothing is to be gained by such high-handedness.

Nevertheless, Wilson's remarks have a serious point if they are interpreted more loosely. Even if brains are not strictly *necessary* for mental events, in our experience the two regularly occur together. So even from this chastened perspective it is important to ask what incorporeal personhood might come to. But the question must be phrased, not in terms of organic brain structure, but in terms of the possibility of personhood in the absence of body. I propose to focus the inquiry by asking, first, what it means to be a person, and especially what sorts of things Christian theism wishes to be able to say of a personal God, and then ask in each case whether it could make sense to say these things of a being who lacks, not only a brain, but any sort of physical body. It will appear that the more we try to understand God's attributes, the more we are brought to a picture of the universe as the body of God (in a sense gradually to become clear) rather than the cosmic monarchical dualism of the traditional picture.

First a note about method. Theologians and philosophers of religion sometimes speak of God as a personal being, but then in their more detailed discussions plunge directly into a consideration of the 'omni-' attributes (omnipotence, omniscience, omnipresence) without further discussion about how these relate to God's nature precisely as personal. Richard Swinburne, for example, considers it fundamental to theism to say that God is personal, and thus begins with an account of what it is to be a person, but having done so, he devotes his attention to concepts like God's creation of the universe, his omnipotence, omniscience, and the like.[3] Of course it is true that theologians have wanted to say these things about God, and that they generate considerable philosophical paradoxes and perplexities. But for this very reason it seems to me to be important not to lose touch with the starting point: it is no use becoming embroiled in a discussion of omnipotence, for instance, without first having shown that an incorporeal being could properly be said to be capable of doing at least *some* things – for if this is impossible, so is omnipotence. The 'omni-' attributes are the very ones which are most puzzling for our concept of personhood, since not even human persons have such capabilities. While there is no question that all our concepts will have to be stretched if they are to apply to God, there is value in starting, not with the stretched form, but with the minimal case, and then extending it where and as philosophical and religious adequacy demands. Thus I propose to begin with perception rather than omniscience, action rather than omnipotence. Initially it will be of great value to see how these more confined concepts develop our understanding of God's personal nature: once we have explored this, we can extend the concepts as appropriate. This approach will help, too, to avoid a discussion of a concept of God who might be a close relative of Aristotle's Unmoved Mover but whose relationship to the God of the faithful is not obvious.

What is a person? This sounds like a Socratic quest for an essence, a quest which even Socrates could not complete. All we need for our purposes, however, is to list some of the characteristics most central to the idea of 'person'. An entity which lacks some of these will have at best attentuated personhood, and if it lacked them all, it could not be called a person. We do not have to decide, however, exactly where the dividing line comes: such a decision may be important for certain legal and moral issues, but for our own investigation a broad sketch is adequate.

Amélie Rorty says: 'The idea of a person is the idea of a unified centre of choice and action, the unit of . . . responsibility.'[4] To be able to choose and act responsibly requires, in turn, rationality and freedom; it also assumes desires or goals, 'projects', so that meaningful choices can be made towards achieving these goals.

3. Richard Swinburne *The Coherence of Theism* pp. 99f.
4. Amélie O. Rorty 'A Literary Postscript' p. 309.

Responsibility is connected, usually, with the notion of others to whom or for whom one is responsible; and a large part of what is normally meant by 'personal' involves relationships with other persons – what some philosophers call 'reciprocity'.[5] These relationships are not purely intellectual in a narrow sense, although the intelligence of the individual is always involved, but are also more or less strongly affective, with love and hate, anger and harmony, hostility, humour, guilt, co-operation, and a host of other emotions and attitudes all playing their part.

Such relationships in turn would be impossible without communication, linguistic and otherwise; and although such communication need not take the form of speech (a severe speech-impediment would not make us classify a brilliant author as sub-personal) it does normally express itself in some variety of language, so that humans are sometimes classified as the language-using animals. Persons, furthermore, individually and together work and play, laugh, and make things; they have creative and aesthetic abilities. This is obviously not an exhaustive account of human personhood; it merely draws attention to some significant aspects of the concept.

We must now ask how these characteristics apply to God. We have already taken note that some modification and stretching will be necessary, and perhaps it will also be important to introduce additional elements. But our central question remains: what do these characteristics, even when modified, teach us about the relationship between God and the physical world? Are they compatible with divine incorporeality? As I have already indicated, I think that an investigation into some of them will lead us rather to think of God embodied; it will advance us considerably in our understanding of what an adequate model of the relationship between God and the world must be like.

Can we say, then, first of all, that God is a 'unified centre of choice and action', and responsible for his activities? Theists would certainly say that we can. Whatever the plans and choices of God with respect to the vast reaches of the universe about which we know nothing, Christians do certainly affirm that God has made choices with regard to humankind: he has chosen to create us, and chooses to sustain us and our environment and thus preserve our existence. He also chooses to reveal himself (communicate with humankind) in various ways. Christians point to the Old Testament stories of his choice of the nation of Israel and of various individuals

5. Cf. Daniel Dennett 'Conditions of Personhood' pp. 175–96.

within it, and above all to the life and death of Jesus of Nazareth as particular ways which God has chosen for his self-revelation. Typically they also maintain that God communicates with them through such activities as prayer and meditation, and through the sacraments. This implies that Christians believe that God has a character, in the above sense of having desires or projects; the divine activities we emphasize most are those projects of his relating to humankind – God's desire for our salvation. Whatever exactly that means, it involves in some sense his desire for our fulfilment and perfection. This shows, also, that God involves himself in relationships, because the fulfilment and perfection of persons which Christians believe God desires cannot be achieved, according to standard teaching, apart from a relationship with himself, a relationship which, as we saw in our discussion of divine immutability, involves not only the human person's rationality and emotions but also God's. In the Scriptures, as we have seen, God's wisdom and God's love, his laughter, his wrath, and his merciful kindness are all exercised towards people and nations in a highly personal way, revealing God's personal involvement, and requiring personal response on the part of the recipients. And Christians today affirm God's creativity and his providence within their intimate relationships with him.

None of this is at all new, although modern theologians are more aware of some of the problems involved than their forebears seemed to be. But how can it be squared with a doctrine of divine incorporeality? In particular, how does God think, or know about the world, and how can he act towards it in the creative, providential and self-communicative ways which lie at the heart of the Christian affirmation that God is love? It will be useful to take one central Christian activity as an example, and see how all the issues come together in a perplexing tangle: let us choose prayer. It is sometimes suggested that the experience of prayer is the key to our learning about God's incorporeality: he can hear and answer prayers of many people in different places simultaneously. But it is not so frequently noticed that the doctrine of incorporeality also raises enormous difficulties for the experience of prayer. As we all know, physical touch plays a crucial role in the communication of human intimacy, yet this is not in any straightforward sense an aspect of our experience of God. And psychological questions apart, how is prayer factually possible if God does not have a body? Without sensory apparatus, how can he hear our prayers? If he is incorporeal, how can he be near us when we pray? How can he be any*where*? If he has no body, how can he act in response?

These three issues: perception and thought, presence, and agency are at the root of the matter. If a being is capable of these, he is conceivably also capable of choices, desires, communication, and many of the other things we normally wish to ascribe to God. Thus we will look at these three basic abilities one by one, to see how they lead us to an understanding of the embodiment of God.

1. Perception and Embodiment

The questions we are raising have been asked before. Anselm of Canterbury, in the eleventh century, was already pondering them. He said:

> But, although it is better for thee to be sensible . . . how art thou sensible, if thou art not a body? . . . For, if only corporeal things are sensible, since the senses encompass a body and are in a body, how art thou sensible, although thou art not a body, but a supreme Spirit, who is superior to body?[6]

Anselm answers these questions in terms of a distinction between the fact and the method of acquiring knowledge. If God as a matter of fact acquires knowledge of colours and tastes, it does not matter that he does not do so by way of 'corporeal sense', that is, by physical sensory apparatus: he can still correctly be said to perceive, though we do not know how.

> Therefore, O Lord, although thou art not a body, yet thou art truly sensible in the highest degree in respect of this, that thou dost cognize all things in the highest degree: and not as an animal cognizes, through a corporeal sense.[7]

But for us, Anselm's answer will not do. We are precisely concerned with whether it would be *possible* for an incorporeal being to 'cognize all things in the highest degree', so the bald statement that God does so cannot be satisfactory. What we need is some account of what it would be like – how it would be a conceptually coherent notion – to have perception without having a body.

Terence Penelhum, in his discussion of the intelligibility of disembodied survival of human persons, attempts to give such an account.

6. Anselm *Proslogium* VI.
7. Ibid.

Beginning with the sense of vision, Penelhum argues that a disembodied person would conceivably be able to have something analogous to our visual perceptions. He would have the experience of objects 'which looked to him as they would look to a normal observer under optimum circumstances from a certain position in space'.[8] He then gives parallel accounts of the other modes of sense-perception: hearing becomes having auditory sensations which an embodied person would have in a given location; touch would be feeling that the object in question was hot or cold, rough or smooth, when it actually was. Thus sense-perception, at least in an attenuated version, would conceivably be possible for an incorporeal person.

However, there is something puzzling about Penelhum's argument here. Vision is defined in terms of how things look from a particular perspective, hearing in terms of how things sound, touch in terms of how things feel. But this seems to beg the question: if what we want to know is whether disembodied vision is possible, then we are asking whether any sense can be given to the expression 'how things look' when predicated of a disembodied person. Do they – can they – 'look' any way at all to him in the absence of any visual apparatus? If they do, then he can see; he has visual perceptions. If not, then we cannot ascribe vision to him. The two stand or fall together, and if the possibility of vision is in question, then so also is the possibility of having any such experiences. The same applies to the other senses.

But a reply is possible. Suppose there is a blind man who has, nevertheless, the ability always to describe the objects of his immediate and more distant environment in terms which neatly correspond to our visual perceptions of them. In such a case, could we deny that he sees them – that is, is he really blind? The answer here depends on how blindness and vision are defined. If they are defined in terms of utilization of normal sense organs, then he is blind (we may suppose for instance that his eyes have been gouged out). If, however, they are defined in terms of the experiences he has, independently of the mechanism for having them, then we would say that he can see – or at least that he has visual experiences. Penelhum's argument is that a disembodied person might conceivably be said to have such visual experiences, and that this might be generalized to the other senses. There is of course still the enormous question of how this could come to be: in the absence of sensory

8. Terence Penelhum *Survival and Disembodied Existence* p. 25.

apparatus, how could such experiences occur? But it is important to notice that the argument has now shifted from a question of logical possibility (which is now conceded) to a question of physical possibility.

Not that this makes the solution obvious. We are now, in fact, very nearly back to Anselm's position, that God, though without sensory apparatus, has all the knowledge which would in the human case require sense organs. But what reason do we have for believing that this might be true? Even if we grant that it is logically conceivable for a blind person to have visual experiences in the sense just described, this does not alter the fact that blind people as a matter of fact do not have them. In the whole of our experience, eyes are necessary for sight (materially, if not logically), ears for hearing, a body for touching. Although we are not compelled by strictly logical considerations to say that this must be the case universally, we have no grounds within our experience for thinking that it is not. It is therefore by no means obvious that we could look forward to disembodied survival as a time when sight will no longer be impeded by our eyes, hearing limited by our ears, or thought by the structure of our brain. Our experience points unequivocally in the opposite direction.

What sense can we make, then, of the idea that God has the sort of knowledge which in our experience would require sense perception? Clearly it is necessary that, if we are to affirm God's personhood, we must also affirm his powers of perception: this part of the dilemma cannot be jettisoned. It is worth remembering the terms in which writers of Scripture describe God's perception: on the most obvious interpretation, they are highly anthropomorphic. 'The Lord's arm is not so short that it cannot save,' writes Isaiah, 'nor his ear too dull to hear; it is your iniquities that raise a barrier between you and your God, because of your sins he has hidden his face so that he does not hear you.' The writer of Leviticus speaks frequently of the food-offering as 'a soothing odour to the Lord', and in other places we have references to God's nostrils. But one of the most religiously satisfying and yet intriguingly inexplicit comments comes from the Psalm writer, who sings:

He that planted the ear, shall he not hear?
He that formed the eye, shall he not see?
He that chastiseth the heathen, shall not he correct?
He that teacheth man knowledge, shall not he know?[9]

9. Psalm 94:9–10 AV.

Whether the apparatus is like our own or not (or whether there might be perception without apparatus) is irrelevant to the poet. What matters to him is that the one who originated our ability to perceive can hardly be without that ability himself; the creator of persons is personal.

From this point it would be possible to proceed in two different directions. One of these, the route I plan to follow, is to question the doctrine of divine incorporeality, and to show that a much less mystifying doctrine of divine perception can be offered on a revised model of the God–world relationship. But the alternative, the 'road not taken', is at least interesting enough for us to take a short glance along it before turning the other way. One could, conceivably, take the doctrine of divine incorporeality as fundamental, and argue that, although we do not know the mechanism, we have plenty of independent reason to believe that God does acquire perceptual knowledge without perceptual apparatus; and since we have already admitted that such apparatus is not logically necessary, we can rest in the assurance that God knows, though we know not how, the things that we would have to learn by way of our sense organs. Provided that we have independent reason to believe that he knows these things – and this is provided by Scripture and continuing religious experience – the method by which he comes to know it need not concern us. And for that matter, is there not an analogy to such non-sensory perception in human clairvoyance, telepathy, and out-of-the-body experiences? As psychical research shows, it is not quite accurate to say that all our experiences of perception require normal sensory apparatus, even though these experiences remain too much of a mystery for us to use as more than examples of inexplicable acquiring of information for which most people would have to use their eyes and ears.

If one did take this approach, it is worth noticing that it has important implications for the doctrine of disembodied survival of human persons. We would not be willing to say that God's perception was in any way less keen than our own, or less accurate; yet on this account it is not dependent on physical organs. Thus if we assume divine incorporeality, we have all the precedent we need for ascribing heightened rather than attenuated perception to human persons who, at death, have been divested of their earthly sensory apparatus; and this is true even though this runs directly counter to our experience of the need for such apparatus if perception is to occur. The same would be true of all other aspects of personhood. If God, though incorporeal, is the supreme paradigm of personhood,

77

then bodies are inessential for human persons after death, even though we cannot imagine this in detail. Philosophers and theologians including Thomas Aquinas sometimes reject dualism as a theory of human persons and argue for resurrection rather than immortality on the grounds that disembodied survival would require an impoverishment rather than an enrichment of perception and personhood generally. If at the same time they believe with Aquinas that God is incorporeal, their arguments are inconsistent.

But I have chosen to push along the other path as far as it will take us. The reason is simple. If we have no experience of perception without embodiment, we are reasonably led to wonder whether a God who has perceptions might also be embodied. An instinctive response is that this is wild anthropomorphism: but if human persons are icons of the divine, then some anthropomorphism is inevitable and proper, and the label of anthropomorphism is not by itself derogatory. It cannot be rejected without a hearing. In the light of what we know about the dependence of perception upon the body in our normal experience of it, it would seem reasonable to ask whether this might not also be true of God.

There is, after all, an important sense in which Penelhum's account of disembodied perception, even if it is adequate for disembodied human beings, would not suffice for the divine case. If visual perception is described as how something would look to an embodied observer, and the location of the disembodied perceiver is defined as that point from which an embodied observer would have such a visual experience, it follows that a disembodied person could only have a limited number of perceptions at a time. He or she could not, for instance, 'see' the north and south faces of Mount Everest simultaneously as each would appear to an embodied person in the ground; let alone objects on both sides of the globe: not, that is, unless he or she were perched on a planet a sufficient distance away and had powers of perception so vastly beyond normal human abilities that even to call it 'perception' is problematic. And yet some such power is just what we want to affirm of God: he can hear prayers simultaneously offered in all parts of the world, and if travel in outer space becomes a way of life, Christians will expect that God will hear their prayers from whatever part of the universe they offer them, nor do they expect to need loudspeakers or radio transmitters. But now it is clear that the model of disembodied perception offered us for making sense of human survival would have to be extended beyond recognition if it is to be an analogue of divine perception.

In some ways, this is just what we would expect. For a theist will affirm that God's perception really is disanalogous to ours in extent and complexity – it must be if God is omniscient – and therefore a model which draws attention to the disproportion is more accurate than one which ignores it. Secondly, a theist might say that, if God is at the place where an embodied person who had the relevant perceptions would be, and if God perceives things on opposite sides of the globe simultaneously, this is just what we need for a doctrine of divine omnipresence. Since God does perceive things from every point of view at once, God is everywhere. With a little manipulating, one might try to make this comport with Thomas Aquinas's comment that 'God exists in everything . . . by presence inasmuch as everything is naked and open to his gaze . . .'[10] – from all possible angles!

But there is another reason for doubting whether Penelhum's account would be adequate for God. The sort of perception he speaks of is most easily understandable if we imagine a disembodied person perceiving apples and oranges, tombstones and trees – 'medium-sized dry goods' such as we constantly perceive in our immediate vicinities. All such perception is, at least in the embodied case, mediated, most obviously by light and sound waves, though other things can also come into play. But we also have perceptions (or perhaps 'awareness' would be a better term) of events taking place *inside* our bodies: we feel hungry, sick, or contented, alert or dull, in pain, or full of well-being. We also have direct awareness of our emotions and our thoughts. Now, God's knowledge of the world and its events has traditionally been held to be more like the latter sort of knowledge than like the former – that is, more like awareness than perception. God's knowledge of the world is direct, unmediated. He does not need light waves to enable him to see what is going on ('the darkness and the light are both alike to thee'); nor do we have to utter the thoughts and intents of our hearts in order for God to hear them. Because God does not require any mediation in his knowledge of the world, it would seem that at least on this count his knowledge is much more closely analogous to the direct awareness we have of our thoughts and feelings than to the indirect knowledge we have of things outside ourselves. But since God has this direct awareness of all things – *no* items of his knowledge about how things are in the world are inferential or

10. Thomas Aquinas *Summa Theologiae* I a, Q 8, art. 3.

mediated – the doctrine of divine omniscience leads us to think of the universe as God's body.

Richard Swinburne, in his discussion of the coherence of the concept of an omnipresent spirit, nearly reaches this conclusion but then backs away from it. He says:

> There is no one place from which God looks out on the world, yet he knows without inference about any state of the world (whether he 'sees' it or 'feels' it we do not know). The traditional theistic view that God has no body has always been supposed to be compatible with the above limited embodiment. The claim that God has no body is the denial of more substantial embodiment, and above all the denial that God controls and knows about the material universe by controlling and getting information from other parts only by being in causal interaction with the former part.[11]

But this latter consideration does not, surely, count against God's having a body but in favour of it – only, his body must be understood as the whole universe, not an individual part of it. The argument clearly does tell against God having a finite Zeus-like body: Zeus presumably did not have this sort of direct knowledge of the world, even though he may have had superhuman means of acquiring information. But God does not need to have a messenger service; he perceives all things directly. Zeus had direct knowledge only of his own self, learned of things around him with his 'far-seeing eye', and had to go to investigate a situation out of visual range of Mount Olympus: Zeus's body was in this respect like ours, and he used it as we use ours to gain new knowledge of the world around us. It would indeed be misguided to think that God had this sort of a body, as though reality could be divided up into the part that is God's body, of which he has direct knowledge, and the part that is not, of which he has only perceptual or inferential knowledge, mediated through some sort of sensory apparatus.

But if God does not have a finite body, does this mean that he is not embodied at all? If we continue the above considerations, this seems to be the wrong way to move. For on this account, the continuum of direct knowledge is proportional to the continuum of embodiment. A disembodied spirit could have direct knowledge only of his or her own thoughts and feelings; all knowledge of the

11. Richard Swinburne pp. 103–4; cf. Jonathon Harrison 'The Embodiment of Mind Or What Use is Having a Body?'

world external to him- or herself would be mediated. An ordinary human being has, in addition to direct knowledge of his or her mental states, direct knowledge of his or her body; but depends on perception and inference for his or her knowledge of the rest of the world. Now, if theists wish to say that God has direct and unmediated knowledge of the whole universe, which typically they do, this seems to point precisely away from a doctrine of divine incorporeality. The theistic alternative to saying that God has a Zeus-like body is not to say that he is incorporeal but to say that the whole universe is his body. Rather than opt for less complete embodiment, as Swinburne advocates, the doctrine of omniscience would push us even further along the embodiment continuum. This would preserve the idea that divine knowledge is unmediated without falling into the difficulty against which Swinburne rightly warns.

However, there are important qualifications which the doctrine of omniscience leads us to make to the idea that God-world relationship is analogous to the person-body relationship. Although we have direct knowledge of our bodies which we do not have of things outside of ourselves – so that, for example, I know where my left hand is without looking for it, even if you have blindfolded me and then moved my hand – there are many complex processes going on inside our bodies of which we have very little knowledge, and the little we have is not direct. For example, I assume that as I write these lines my central nervous system is operating in complex ways; but although this is happening inside me, I have only very fragmentary notions of what is going on, and even these are not gained directly, but are acquired by reading books and poring over diagrams prepared by neurophysiologists who have never examined my brain, only others which they believe are relevantly similar. But all God's knowledge is direct; it is analogous to my knowledge of my conscious thoughts and sensations, not to my gleanings from medical textbooks. Thus if we think of the world as God's body, we must think of it as a body of which he has immediate knowledge of all its parts and processes.

Although this is a disanalogy with our awareness of our bodies, however, it is a disanalogy which continues to point away from the idea that God is incorporeal. As we have already seen, an incorporeal being would not have direct knowledge of any body. We have it, in part, of our own bodies. God has direct knowledge of the whole universe. The continuum points in the direction of what we might call more thoroughgoing embodiment in the case of God – of God being, literally, 'more in touch' with his body than we are

81

with ours – rather than towards more limited embodiment. The disanalogy strengthens the case for divine embodiment rather than weakens it.

This model seems fairly plausible as long as we restrict ourselves to speaking of knowledge, for theists do want to say that God knows whatever we know (and a great deal more) and that he knows it directly. But when we turn from the cognitive side of things and think about emotions and sensations, the theory is at first sight less attractive. Must God feel whatever I feel? If I am in pain, it is in line with theism to say that God knows and understands about my distress, but must God actually *feel* it? After all, we have direct knowledge of such sensations precisely because we feel them, not because of cognitive processes. Does God feel the world the way we feel our bodies? Swinburne rejects such a suggestion: 'There is no material object in which disturbances cause God pains; nor any material object whose state affects the way in which God thinks about the world,'[12] analogous to the way that getting alcohol into my body makes me see double.

Perhaps not. But before ceding the point, it is worth asking why not. If no disturbances in the universe can cause God pain, is this because it is *a priori* impossible for God to feel pain? Why? – Because he is a spirit, and only bodies feel pains? But that begs the question, for if we were to say that God is embodied in the world, then perhaps he could feel pains. The fact that we are not used to speaking in such terms cannot itself be an objection. Perhaps someone would say that God could not have pains because that would violate the doctrine of immutability. But we have already examined that doctrine and found it wanting: the God of the prophets and apostles, mystics and martyrs, is changeless in character, but is powerful to act on behalf of those who call upon him.

I suspect that there are two reasons why theologians have been so reluctant to ascribe direct sensations, whether pain or any other sort, to God. The first is that most of our sensations are too *trivial* to apply to God. If God felt every twinge and tickle which I feel, as well as those of everybody else, not to mention all the animals and everything else in the universe which might give God sensations if the universe is in some sense his body – does not the hypothesis crumble under its own silliness? In reply, however, I suggest, first, that if one used parallel reasoning, the completely orthodox notion of omniscience would look just as silly. Must we really say that God

12. Swinburne, pp. 103–4.

keeps count of the exact number of gnats in each part of the continent of Africa and knows their precise location? Does he keep track of every particle of dust as it whirls in the intergalactic spaces? The idea that God feels every sensation of the universe is no more ridiculous than the idea that God knows every possible item of data: omniscience pushed to this extreme looks equally foolish.

But surely in both cases pushing it this way is mistaken. What is religiously important about the doctrine of omniscience is not that God is like a gigantic computer who has stored all facts (and all possibilities) in an infinite list of data, much of it trivial, but rather that God has intimate personal knowledge of each of us and our circumstances: his *understanding* (not his data-retrieval ability) is infinite. But if it is because of God's kindness and individual care that we find comfort in the thought that 'the very hairs of our heads are all numbered' – and not because of a fetish about statistical data relating to baldness – is it not similarly consoling to think that God could be 'touched with the feeling of our infirmities'?

Of course it is silly to think that God feels all our sensations if by that we mean that he pays endless attention to things we hardly notice – but that is a parallel silliness to thinking that omniscience requires that God meticulously stores up the knowledge of exactly how many molecules are discarded when people file their fingernails. However when we think of the things that are really important to us – long-term struggle against depression, or chronic severe discomfort – it becomes far more significant that God should understand our feelings, not just in the sense of knowing about them from some lofty untouched plane like an eternal bystander, but really sympathizing, 'feeling with us'. God's understanding of us, his intimate sharing of our joys and pains, is more credible to us on the model of the world as God's body, giving him, therefore, immediate sensations as well as direct knowledge, than on the model that God is spirit, utterly removed from ever feeling anything analogous to our suffering.

There is, however, a difference between sympathizing with someone's pain and having that pain oneself; if you break your leg in a skiing accident I can sympathize even though my own leg is unhurt. Indeed, if my leg were also broken, or if I somehow directly felt the pain in your leg, I might be feeling so sorry for myself that I would have no sympathy left over for you. So why should we say that God actually feels our pains, rather than that he sympathizes with them?

One reason we might wish to do so emerges when we look more

closely at what it is to sympathize with someone. To sympathize, one need not actually have someone else's pain, but one must have had a relevantly similar pain at some time. A person who has enjoyed continuously robust health finds it very difficult to sympathize with the depression of an invalid, and can do so only by a strong effort of the imagination extrapolating from whatever brief indispositions he has had. A person in deep bereavement prefers the company of someone who has suffered a similar grief. Thus if God sympathizes with us, it is more helpful to suppose that he has sensations than that he does not, for if he does not, he could never have experienced anything like our pain. Only a God who can suffer could command respect after Auschwitz.

But if the universe is in this sense God's body, and we are all parts of the universe, then are we not all parts of a single body? If that is so, how is it that we are relatively independent of one another – why, for example, do we not literally feel one another's pains? This seems to land us in a whole web of confusions, for as we have seen, normally we would say that one way of telling people apart is the very fact that we have different bodies; to speak now as though we are all part of one body is unclear on many counts. The difficulties here, however, are part of the larger difficulty of divine sovereignty and human individuality, and rather than try to deal with the puzzles piecemeal, I propose to defer the remainder of this discussion to Chapter 7.

There is, however, another problem with the idea that God could have direct sensations. If our physical sensations are often too trivial for us to pay attention to, they are also, sometimes, incapacitating. The severity of prolonged intense physical pain or psychic distress often alters a personality in destructive ways, and is usually a detriment to clear thinking and acting. Yet we would hardly want to say that God is incapacitated by earthquakes or that his character is changed by volcanic eruptions.

But this problem can be briefly dealt with. A theist, whatever his model of the relationship between God and the world, must maintain that, to put it crudely, God can cope with more than we can. If God can hear thousands of prayers simultaneously and respond appropriately to them all, it is no great extension of the point to say that his understanding of his children involves feeling with them, individually, yet without being utterly overwhelmed by their feelings, even when they themselves are. Perhaps part of what we mean by praising God for his steadfastness is thankfulness that he *can* cope with more than we do, that his 'personality', his dispositions towards us, his kindness and purposes do not change, even though he takes our suffering and our sorrow upon himself.

It is indeed remarkable that, in the light of biblical teaching about the love and involvement of God with persons, the best revelation of which is Jesus of Nazareth who voluntarily takes upon himself suffering to the point of death and sympathizes with pain and anguish as no one else has done, Christian theologians have been so reluctant to say that God could feel pain. It is the idea of an aloof eternal bystander, a monarch looking down upon his pitiful kingdom without feeling its miseries, which is revolting to Christian belief, not an idea of the involvement of God with suffering and sorrow. Picturing the universe as God's body gives us a model more suited to describe this vital aspect of Christian theology than the model of cosmic dualism.

2. Action and Embodiment

A parallel argument to that given with regard to perception can be constructed, which shows that the idea of God's *action* on the world also makes more sense on the model that the world is God's body than on the traditional model. In order for us to act on the world, it is normally necessary for us to use an indirect method, originating in a movement of our own bodies. For example, if I wish to move a pen, I do so by moving my hand first. However, there are certain actions which I can do *without* doing anything else first; these are the direct actions of my own body. I do not have to do anything first, before I can move my hand. This latter sort of action, requiring no antecedent, has been called a 'basic action'.[13] Unless we can perform basic actions, we cannot do anything else either; all our action on the world begins with a movement of our bodies.

Now, a disembodied person would not have a body to move, and therefore could perform no basic actions. But then how can he get any action on the world started? Perhaps an appeal might be made to telekinesis – direct movement of a physical object at a distance, with no perceptible intervening mechanism. But as Anthony Kenny has pointed out, this is not really an analogue to the case of the disembodied agent, because the agent who claims paranormal ability is still an otherwise normal embodied person performing basic actions in other contexts. Indeed, if this were not the case, if we suspected that not even the movements of his own body were

13. Arthur Danto 'Basic Actions'.

basic actions, then we would not be willing to say that he was the real agent of the paranormal activity.[14]

Now, just as theists wish to affirm that God's knowledge of the world is direct and immediate, they similarly wish to say that God can *act* directly, without any intervening action or mechanism: God did not wiggle his fingers to cause a mechanism to operate which sent fire from heaven to consume Elijah's sacrifice on Mount Carmel; he 'spake and it was done'. But in terms of the present discussion, this means that any action of God on the world is a basic action: he does not have to do anything else first. Terence Penelhum, discussing the action of disembodied spirits, says that if they can act at all, they do so, not by means of mechanisms, but directly: if a spirit raises a table, then the raising of the table is a basic action for the spirit. But then we might as well say that, at least for purposes of that action, the table has become the body of the spirit.[15] In the case of God, the conclusion to be drawn is spelled out by Kenny:

> If God can act in the world directly and without intermediary, as traditionally he has been held to, then on Danto's definition the world would be God's body. Most traditional theologians would have rejected this idea with horror.[16]

But would they? This seems to me to be too strong. It is true, of course, that most traditional theologians would not have expressed themselves in this way, because for various reasons, some of which we have already seen, they considered it more important to stress the disanalogies between God and material bodies. Throughout the Middle Ages, matter was conceived of as utterly inert; after the Enlightenment bodies were thought of as analogous to the interrelation of mechanistic clockwork: with such views of matter (which we will look at more closely later) it was of course important to insist that God was not material. But as Swinburne points out, when we think of God's interaction with the physical world:

> It is important . . . not to overemphasize the extent of God's nonembodiment in the view of traditional theism. . . . The view of traditional theism is that in many ways God is not related to a material object as a person is to his body, but in other ways he is so related.[17]

14. Anthony Kenny *The God of the Philosophers* p. 126.
15. Terence Penelhum p. 42.
16. Anthony Kenny p. 126.
17. Richard Swinburne p. 107.

In terms of his action on the world in particular, Swinburne argues that God is related to physical reality as a person is related to his body, in just the way that Kenny implies would have been repudiated by traditional theologians.

There are, however, also disanalogies, parallel to those we encountered in our discussion of divine knowledge. In the first place, a human person can perform only a limited range of basic actions, and a great many of the things he does are not basic, even if they must be initiated by basic actions. Whenever human action involves the movement of some things other than the person's own body, non-basic, indirect action is initiated by direct, basic action. But a theist wants to say that all God's actions on the world are direct and basic; he never has to do anything first to accomplish his purposes, but does everything directly, without intervening apparatus. This would, indeed, be incompatible with the hypothesis that God has a finite body like our own, and lives on some planet of a distant galaxy from which he keeps his fingers on the control panel of the universe – if that were what was meant by having a body, then obviously God does not have one. But our considerations have already pushed us well away from such a view. What is important is that the direction of the push is not towards more restricted embodiment, as Swinburne suggests, but rather towards a concept of more complete embodiment. There are difficulties with the notion that an incorporeal spirit could perform any basic actions whatsoever which would result in physical movement; on the other hand, God can perform any physical action, and any such action on God's part is direct, basic. Just as in the discussion of divine perception, therefore, so here too we are led to the conclusion that the logical alternative to saying that God does not have a finite body is not to say that he is utterly incorporeal, but rather to say that the whole world is God's body. There is more than one alternative to the hypothesis that God has a finite body like a superman; thus to show the absurdity of such a concept of God does not rule out the attractiveness of divine embodiment.

Furthermore, just as we saw in the case of divine perception, God's control of the universe, like his awareness of it, is far more extensive than our awareness or our control of our own bodies. Much of the movement of our bodies is movement of which we are not even aware, let alone movement which we can voluntarily control. Most of us, for example, have very little idea of how our livers function, and although we can to a certain extent influence that function by what we eat and drink, we cannot bring it under deliberate control in any direct way. But just as an omniscient God must be aware of all parts of the universe, so an omnipotent God must be in direct control of all parts of it. Although this is disanalogous to our control over our bodies, however, this is once again not a disanalogy which would push us back towards saying that God is incorporeal, but rather forward to an idea of more complete embodiment.

It is worth pausing to be clear about the term 'complete embodiment'. Obviously I do not mean that *more* of God is embodied (that there is less spirit 'left over') than is the case with humans: we have already seen how inadequate dualism is for a theological understanding of human persons, and our aim is to see to what extent a holistic model of human personhood is helpful for understanding the relationship between God and the world. Rather, I am contrasting the *degree* of deliberate knowledge and control that God has over the universe with the degree of knowledge and control that we have over our own bodies. Our bodies and their movements are to a very large extent independent of our desires and choices: the heart beats, the blood circulates without attention or will, nor is it through any choice of our own that we have hearts in the first place. There is a givenness about our bodies and their movements; consequently it is inappropriate to refer to their involuntary movements as basic actions, because strictly speaking, they are not *actions* at all.

But according to theological tradition, God is in immediate direct control of the whole universe; all of its movements are, in this sense, his basic actions. If we were to draw a scale showing the relative number of actions and movements of different sorts of entities which could be labelled 'basic', an incorporeal spirit would have fewest, an embodied person would have more, and God would have most – this is what I mean by saying that God is more completely embodied than human persons. The differences between his actions and the involuntariness of many of our bodily movements is not a difference which pushes us in the direction of incorporeality but just the opposite: we acknowledge much more complete voluntary control on God's part than on our own. The moves here are parallel to those in the argument about divine knowledge in the previous section.

The idea that the universe is God's body and that all his actions are basic actions raises two large problems: the problem of evil, and a problem about natural law. Starting with the latter, how can we say that God is in continuous voluntary control of the whole of his body, the universe, if the universe displays the uniformity and causal regularity which makes it discoverable by the physical sciences? It would seem that either the natural laws which scientists have painstakingly discovered are unreliable, or else God does not have the voluntary control of the universe after all.

This dilemma, however, need not detain for long a theologian who believes that the world is God's body. It is easiest to see this by remembering what we would say about natural law if we hold that God is *not* corporeal. If God were a spirit, separate from the material world, we would account for natural law and the causal chain by saying that this is the way in which God deliberately organized the world and sustains it in being. If God is omnipotent, then he is perfectly free to change the natural laws if he chooses: he could, for example, change the rate of rotation of the earth if he wished to do so. Of course, that would have devastating consequences for us, and we trust God not to do it, but that has nothing to do with whether God is *powerful* enough to intervene in existing natural law. A theist after all maintains that in some sense God brought these causal regularities into being in the first place. If he wished to, he could change any or all of them in ways we cannot even conceive of (though of course we might not survive to discover the new causal regularities or lack of them). Thus on the traditional view of cosmic dualism, the uniformity of nature is not a logical necessity but a product of God's free choice, in both origin and duration: in traditional language, God freely creates and sustains the world and its regularities, though he is under no compulsion to do so.

I suggest that we can say just the same things of the world as God's body. If we assume, as I have argued, that God has complete control over all parts of his body all the time, then we can say that God has deliberately arranged it in the way it now is. Of course there is nothing (logically) to prevent him from changing its present organization except his own steadfast purposes; but that is true of the traditional view as well. Neither view makes God subject to natural law; both attribute the continuing uniformity of nature to his sustaining will. On either view, the laws of nature hold and are reliable because God has set them up in the first place and continually preserves them rather than interferes with their regularity; but by the same token, an omnipotent God is not bound by the regularities of nature if he should choose not to be: God *could* cause 'the sun to be darkened and the moon be turned to blood'. We can have confidence in scientific method, discovery and prediction, not because, like Deists, we believe that God has nothing to do with the ongoing course of the world, but because we believe that he is not arbitrary: he will continue to sustain the universe. But he does not have to: he chooses to. The danger of the cosmic dualism model in this connection is that it allows us to slip too easily into thinking of the universe and its laws as somehow independent of the ongoing sustenance of God: the model of the universe as the embodiment of God underscores the continuous dependence of the universe on his voluntary sustaining power.

Such a model also has the advantage of illuminating the notions of providence and miracle. If the world is God's body, and every part of it is sustained by his will, then he can arrange the natural order to suit his purposes (providence) and alter it in individual 'miraculous' instances if he so chooses. Whether he ever *would* so choose to interrupt the causal sequence which he has ordained is of course an open question on this view as on any other, but at least we would not be tempted to think of some kind of monarch in the sky reaching down to intervene in the causal sequence: nor does this view encourage a 'god-of-the-gaps' theology. The idea of the universe as the embodiment of God provides in these respects a religiously and philosophically satisfying picture of God's actions in the world in a way that is compatible with continuing scientific endeavour. The whole unfolding of nature, including at least to some degree humankind's part in it, will be the manifestation of divine activity. This does not mean that there can be no particularity in God's action: some events and processes, notably those surrounding the life and death of Jesus of Nazareth, can properly be seen as more revelatory of God than other events, just as some actions of a person are more significant than others for an estimate of his or her character. But this view does render unnecessary any concept of miracles which sees them as interventions from 'out there' by some monarchical deity after the order of Zeus – a concept which many theologians would in any case abandon with relief.

But what can we say about the problem of evil? If every event in the universe is to be understood as willed by God – indeed, if the laws of nature are best understood as the regular activity of his body in his conscious control – then it follows that God not only permits hurricanes and earthquakes, he actually performs them and is responsible for all their destructive consequences. It was bad enough, on the traditional model, to have to say that God allows evil; but if God actually brings it about, is any theodicy possible?

But that is a misleading way of putting the problem. On any

view of the relationship between God and the operation of nature, God organizes the universe into natural laws – consistent patterns of behaviour, we might say – which, because of their consistency, can be said to have a quasi-autonomous status. In the course of this semi-independent nature, earthquakes and other physical disasters are bound to occur, but these are then seen as the natural consequences of a causal system which is on the whole good, rather than as direct performances of God. Thus to the extent that the 'evilness' of these occurrences is mitigated by the fact that they are natural outworkings of the causal sequence, this response is open to the theologian who pursues the model of divine embodiment. As we have seen, a theist who takes this approach can be just as committed to the findings of science and the regularities of nature as a cosmic dualist is. If these regularities are in general good, even though they sometimes result in human and animal suffering, then one who believes that the universe is the embodiment of God can appeal to the inappropriateness of frequent divine intervention as readily as can a traditional theist. I am not suggesting that the problem of evil is not really a problem, nor even that an appeal to the regularities of nature can help to solve it. I am only saying that it is not a greater or even a different problem for this view than for a cosmic dualist; there is recourse to just the same sort of appeals in attempting to construct a theodicy. All the moves open to a traditional theist in constructing a theodicy are equally open to one who says that the world is God's body: he can appeal to the overriding goodness of regularities in natural law, to the free will of persons, and to the idea of the world as a vale of soul-making. And in addition he can say that, if the world is God's body, then although God is ultimately responsible for all our suffering, in another sense he shares it, he feels it with us in a more literal sense than would be possible for a cosmic dualist to affirm.

But if the world is God's body, then must we not say that there is evil *in* God himself – God containing evil? It is one thing to say that God permits evil and that he is ultimately responsible for it, but that is different from saying that God himself is evil. Yet if we say that the world is God's body, then the evil in the world appears to be evil in God – and how, then, can God be perfectly good?

From what I have already said, however, it is clear that this objection rests on taking the distinction between God and the world even in traditional theism too strongly. As we shall see in more detail in a later chapter, there is a sense in which any theist must affirm that all reality is from God: belief in creation *ex nihilo* is not the belief that the universe somehow owes its existence to something other than God, namely nothing, out of which God created it. Unless one is willing to adopt a Manichaean view, in which the material universe is irreducibly other than God, one must affirm that in some sense 'God is All', all things have their origin in God, and hence evil itself is in God. One simple way of pointing to *what* sense this has is just to recall that, if God were somehow to cease to exist, so would everything else, including evil. In that sense the universe and everything in it, evil not excepted, has no independent existence apart from God.

One of the most profound struggles with the problem of evil in Christian thought can be found in the writings of the Protestant mystic Jakob Boehme – profound because he takes just this point very seriously. Boehme's ideas are sometimes dismissed as an aberration; he is thought of as an obscure and heterodox curiosity. But though he is obscure and possibly heterodox, he should not be lightly dismissed, especially since his thought has been an influence on major twentieth-century theologians.[18] Boehme says:

> God is all. He is darkness and light, love and wrath, fire and light.
> For all things have their first beginning from the outflow of the divine will, be it evil or good, love or sorrow.[19]

The conflict between darkness and light, good and evil, which Boehme finds in the natural world and poignantly in human persons cannot have any origin except God himself, and must therefore somehow be a reflection of him. Hell itself cannot ultimately be outside of an omnipresent God.

But although I think that we must take Boehme's point seriously that ultimately nothing, not even evil itself, could exist without God, and hence that in that sense God is the origin of evil and evil is in God, we can make a distinction between saying that evil is in God and that God himself is evil. God is evil only if, to use a Kantian notion, he has an evil will: that is, if there is nothing to justify the evil for which he is ultimately responsible and which could not exist but for him. If a theodicy can be provided, whether in terms of a free-will defence or some other explanation of how evil is a necessary condition for bringing about God's good purposes, then we cannot say that God is evil. No special problem is raised by saying that

18. For instance Paul Tillich, who wrote the preface to John Joseph Stoudt's book on Boehme, *Sunrise to Eternity*.
19. Jakob Boehme *The Way to Christ* 4.2.9; 7.1.23.

the world is God's body. Although the 'in' in 'evil is in God' can then be taken literally (that is, spatially), this does not collapse the distinction between the statement, which all Christians must accept, that evil is finally ontologically dependent upon God, and the statement that God himself is evil, which means that he deliberately produces or allows evil without justification. Only if this distinction were collapsed would this be an objection to saying that the world is God's body.

I wish to emphasize that I do not think this to be any answer to the problems of evil in general. I do not even know whether such an answer is possible. But my point is that, if it is possible for cosmic dualism, then it is equally possible, on exactly the same lines, for one who sees the world as God's body. No special problems are raised; the new model leaves the problem of evil just where it was before. We will return to it when we examine the doctrine of creation and its significance for a theist who believes that God and the world are one reality, not two.

3. Omnipresence and Embodiment

There is a sense in which the doctrine of God's omnipresence is the heart of Christian theism. Unless God is present everywhere at all times, how could he know all that occurred or be in control of it? How could we be sure that he heard our prayers and had not deserted us in times of crisis? If God were not omnipresent, our relationship with him would be much more problematic. This is brought out in a striking way by the Old Testament story of Elijah's contest with the prophets of Baal. When their God did not send down fire from heaven in response to their prayers, Elijah taunted them to 'Call louder, for he is a god; it may be he is deep in thought, or engaged, or on a journey; or he may have gone to sleep and must be woken up.' The test of religious truth, in the context of this story, is not an intellectual assessment of competing claims; it is rather decided by watching to see which God responds – which God is actually present to his devotees. A god who is engaged or on a journey, and thus not present to those who pray to him, is not a god at all; nor will it do to say that he was deep in thought or even that he was busy answering someone else's prayers. To be a God, he must be able to respond to all prayers at once; he must be omnipresent.

It is often thought that the doctrine of omnipresence is in direct contradiction to the idea that God has a body. God must be present everywhere, and an embodied being could not be everywhere, since 'body' entails spatial locality. Thus God could not have a body. Now, the direction of our investigation might lead us to suppose that if it could be shown that the whole universe is God's body, then that objection could be overcome: if God's body is infinitely big, then he is omnipresent. However, I think that both these responses betray inadequate reflection on the concept of God's presence, an inadequacy which is regrettable in view of the religious significance of that concept.

We might consider first of all the claim that omnipresence would be incompatible with having a body of finite size, and would thus by itself rule out the idea that God is a being among beings. The issues will be clarified if we use an example of the presence of a human person, and then return to the case of divine presence. We may begin by asking what the relationship is between where a person's body is and where he is present. It is obvious that there is some relationship between St Francis being present in the bishop's court in Assisi and his body being there: one could hardly say that he was present there even though his body was in the church of San Damiano. What exactly this relationship is (and whether it could for some purposes be replaced by, say, two-way television) we can for the moment leave aside. What is important, however, is that although there is a significant relationship between where St Francis' body is and where he is, the relationship is not such that he is present only in the particular volume of space occupied by his body.

It is so natural for us to see that there is a clear relationship between where we are present and where our bodies are locatable, that it is easy for us to neglect other aspects of the notion of presence. Although it is indeed necessary for St Francis to be physically present in Assisi (that is, his body must occupy a certain volume of space within the town walls) in order for it to be correct to say that he is present there, he is not present only within the spatio-temporal co-ordinates which specify the location of his body. If he could be said to be present at the inquiry before the Bishop of Assisi, for instance, it is at least in part because he knew what was going on and could in some measure influence it. It is true that for him to be present in the bishop's palace, he must have been *bodily* present, but from this it does not follow that his body must be in all parts of the palace court or that he was present in no part of the palace except the volume occupied by his body: he did not have to be in actual physical contact with all the people to whom he was present. Whatever are the necessary and sufficient conditions for

94

saying that someone is present in a certain place, it is apparent that the notion of presence cannot be so restricted that one could correctly be said to be present only inside one's skin: St Francis was embarrassingly present to all who were in that court, though clearly his body did not permeate the whole of it nor did he physically touch all who heard him.

The point becomes clearer when we notice that 'presence' is a notion applicable in its strict sense to persons, not to inanimate objects. The candles and crozier in the bishop's courtroom obviously occupied a certain amount of the space of the room, but it would be an odd use of language to say that they were present at St Francis' speech. And what if St Francis himself, weary from building the church at San Damiano, dropped off to sleep while his father was haranguing the bishop, and remained sleeping soundly for the whole discussion that followed. Was he then present at that discussion? Would it not have been at least as accurate to describe him as present if, although his body was actually elsewhere, there was two-way television communication between him and the bishop's palace, by means of which he listened and replied in an alert and influential manner? Whatever we may say about these border-line cases (and a decision about them is not crucial for the main point) it is at least clear that when St Francis rises, strips himself of his rich clothing, and begins to speak, he is present to all who listen and observe. All the hearers, whatever the exact spatial relationships between his place and theirs in the court, are in his presence – though clearly he does not come into actual physical contact with all of them or somehow permeate the space surrounding them. The presence of a person, then, is not simply a matter of the spatio-temporal co-ordinates which demarcate the volume of space occupied by that person's body: it involves some such personal things as consciousness and awareness, and perhaps the ability to influence the course of events.

Let us now apply all of this to our consideration of God's omnipresence and the objection that, if God were embodied, such omnipresence would be impossible. If God had a body which was spatially located somewhere in the universe, and if, from that position, he knew everything that is going on in the universe and was able to influence it all, on what grounds could his omnipresence be denied? If St Francis was present in the bishop's court, and not only in the spatio-temporal co-ordinates of the court which were occupied by the volume of his body, then by parallel reasoning there is no need to assert either that God would have to be incorporeal or that he would have to have an infinitely big body in order for him to be omnipresent. What is required for omnipresence is not incorporeality *or* permeation of all space but awareness and the ability to influence all parts of the universe – perhaps on analogy with Big Brother in Orwell's *1984* on a grander (and rather more benevolent) scale.

Thus we could say that God is present in the universe if his body is located somewhere in the universe with at least as much justification as if his body is the whole of the universe or if he is incorporeal. If we were to confine the notion of presence so much that God must be incorporeal or infinitely huge to be said to be omnipresent, then we must also say that we are present only inside our skins – and that, as we have seen, is unacceptable. To uphold the doctrine that God is omnipresent with respect to the universe, all that is necessary is that he is aware of every aspect of the universe and that he can influence it; it is not necessary that he must permeate the whole of it. It now becomes clear that anyone who thought that omnipresence was a sort of permeation would have a very difficult time making sense of divine incorporeality, for how could a wholly non-spatial being properly be said to be any*where*? And to say that a spirit, since it is non-spatial, could not be anywhere – since spatial co-ordinates could not be applicable – but that he could be everywhere seems even more confused. This might be taken as an argument in support of the model of the world as God's body, but that would be too hasty. The point is rather that omnipresence is a different concept from permeation, whether 'spiritual' or physical.

The classical biblical expression of omnipresence, indeed, invites interpretation in the sense, not of permeation, but of loving awareness and ability to intervene:

> Lord, thou hast examined me and knowest me.
> Thou knowest all, whether I sit down or rise up . . .
> Where can I escape from thy spirit? Where can I flee from thy Presence?
> If I climb up to heaven, thou art there;
> If I make my bed in Sheol, again I find thee.
> If I take my flight to the frontiers of the morning or dwell at the limit of the western sea,
> Even there thy hand will meet me and thy right hand will hold me fast.[20]

20. Psalm 139:7–10 NEB.

What is of crucial importance to the Jewish writers reflecting on God's presence is not incorporeality or permeation but the assurance that God will not go to sleep; his loving watchful care over his people continues at all times.

> The guardian of Israel never slumbers, never sleeps.
> The Lord is your guardian, your defence at your right
>   hand . . .
> The Lord will guard you against all evil;
> He will guard you, body and soul.[21]

What this comes to is the conclusion that the doctrine of omnipresence is vitally related to the doctrines of omnipotence and omniscience, and hence to our understanding of God's perception and agency. But as we have already seen, these can best be understood if we think of the world as God's body. The doctrine of the presence of God, taken by itself, does not require that God must permeate all space, and hence does not entail that the world is God's body, as might at first have been supposed. But omnipresence does entail universal perception and agency, and thus in an indirect way supports the suggested model of divine embodiment. But this is because of the belief that God's knowledge and God's actions are basic and unmediated, like a person's movement and knowledge of his own sensations, not because of an unreflective confusion of the concept of presence with the idea of occupation of spatio-temporal co-ordinates.

The difference between omnipresence and omni-permeation can be brought out more fully by further reflection upon the religious significance of God's presence. If omnipresence were understood merely as omni-permeation, then much of what Christians wish to indicate by it would become very problematical: it means something much deeper, more 'religious', than can be grasped by mere discussion of spatio-temporal co-ordinates. This can be brought out by noticing that, while Christians do indeed affirm a general doctrine of omnipresence, they also specify God's presence in more particular ways: they think of what we might roughly call 'degrees' of presence. Thus God is more truly present in a person than in a lamp-post, in an act of mercy than in an act of terrorism, in the Bible than in *The Times*, in the Blessed Sacrament than in a rock or a brick – even though in *some* sense he is present in them all. Thus, taken in

21. Psalm 121:4–7 NEB.

religious terms, the doctrine of omnipresence has far more to do with grace and immanence than with spatial permeation.

If we think of the universe as God's body, it is possible to make sense of this religious requirement. Although God is omnipresent, in the sense of having direct understanding and control of all that occurs, some occurrences, as we have seen, are far more revelatory of him – and thus communicate his presence more powerfully – than others do, just as some of a person's activities reveal his personality more than others do. For example, a letter to a friend will normally be more revelatory of a person than a shopping list he writes, though a detective or a psychiatrist might be able to discern a great deal about the person even from the shopping list. Thus also the Bible could be taken as more revelatory of God than *The Times*, even though both ultimately depend on him for their existence, and a person who knows how might be able to discern something of the nature of God from a perusal of the latter: at least Christians would not want to rule this out. Although God is present everywhere, certain situations and occurrences bring him more to our attention than others do, as though a person who has been sitting silently in a room suddenly begins to speak. He was there all along, but his speaking makes us notice him, makes him present to us.

There is, of course, also a disanalogy between God's revelatory presence and the presence of a person revealed through his activities. Part of the reason that some activities of a person are more revelatory of him than others is that persons have only limited freedom. Thus the fact that a person eats or drinks or sleeps does not reveal anything about him personally which makes him different from anybody else (even though what or how he eats or drinks may be significant) although it does say something about the whole human race of which he is a member. But in the case of God, all actions are free; none are required by theological necessity. Even the regularities which we call natural law are not binding upon him; as we have seen, he could change them if he wished to. Thus one of the grounds for differentiating the degrees of revelatoriness of a person's behaviour is removed in the case of God: we cannot think that any of God's actions are less deliberate or less free than any others.

But what follows from this? Only that, if we had perfect understanding, we should be able to interpret everything that happened in terms of its relationship to God. We should be able to see how each event showed God's character – whether his patience and mercy or his generosity and good humour. But this is not very helpful. If we had perfect understanding we should comprehend God's purpose in everything – but obviously we *don't*. And because we don't, we often cannot discern just how a given event is revelatory of God: how are we to take a particular shower of rain, for instance? As a miraculous answer to a farmer's prayers, or as the outcome of natural laws independent of his prayers? In either case, it would be revelatory of God, but *what* it would reveal is different in the former case than in the latter.

This shows that 'reveals' is an ambiguous word. There is one sense in which everything – even evil – somehow reveals God. But there is another sense in which revelation requires that the message has been correctly understood – if it has not, then revelation has not fully taken place. A given set of statements, for example (a 'communication') may or may not communicate; that is, it may not be understood as intended. This is not entirely at random, of course; it depends on the background of the communicants, their language, vocabulary, frame of reference, past experiences, and so on. Thus, although in one sense all of the things that happen reveal God, in another sense some of his actions are much more revelatory than others; we understand something of him through them; communication is successful.

Nor is there any reason to think that this is accidental. If Christianity is true, then God chooses to reveal himself in particular ways to particular people and groups – ways which might not have been effective had the background of people been different. What would the shepherds of the Christmas story have made of the star which had such significance for the Magi? Christian theology holds that God relates to people, not abstractly, but in the concrete events of their history and particular circumstances, giving increasing knowledge of himself. Thus for instance the early Fathers interpreted the whole Old Testament history as a preparation for the coming of Christ, the culmination of its revelation. Whether they were correct in this interpretation is of course another question; the flawed nature of the recipient always makes his interpretation fallible. But the point is that although in one sense all things reveal God – God is their omnipresent creator and sustainer – in another sense we can speak of degrees of presence, for we can grasp and be grasped by his revelation more in some contexts than in others, in the light of which the whole of experience can then be better understood. Thus a sacramental view of the universe does not preclude, but rather presupposes, special sacraments, for unless there were specific situa-

99

tions in which God's presence was mediated we should hardly know what to make of the general case.

This is not by itself a decisive argument for divine embodiment: any model of the relationship between God and the world which takes seriously the doctrines of creation and providence is open to this view of revelation and the sacraments. But if we have reason to think of the world as God's body, as we have seen from the concepts of perception and agency, we can see that the doctrine of omnipresence, both in its general sense and in its religiously significant sense of God's presence mediated in revelation and sacrament, comports well with this new model.

6

The Transcendence of an Embodied God

One of the most decisive considerations for the early theologians of the Christian Church was that, whatever model is used of God, God is not to be identified with the universe or any part of it because God is transcendent, infinite and unlimited. As we have already seen, the Fathers for the most part repudiated the Stoic identification of God with the material universe; in early modern times Spinoza's *Deus sive natura* was considered heterodox for much the same reasons. If God and the universe are one reality, not two, then is not God limited, finite, and indeed subject to the laws of matter? Such a view of God is so obviously inadequate that it would hardly seem to warrant closer inspection.

And yet in the previous chapter we have seen that the divine attributes of omnipotence, omniscience and omnipresence can be understood as well or better on a theological model of the world as God's body; furthermore, metaphysical dualism is a notoriously difficult position to defend, and as we have noted, the problems are not diminished if one is trying to defend it on a cosmic scale. This of course does not make it false; a doctrine may be true without being either easy or fashionable. Nevertheless our findings up to this point should prompt us to look again at the doctrines of transcendence and infinity, to see whether they too might be illuminated by the model of the universe as the embodiment of God.

There is good reason to reconsider the traditional view. In the various formulations of orthodox doctrine, the doctrine of divine transcendence has been balanced, sometimes rather precariously, against the doctrine of divine immanence. Now it is easy so to qualify transcendence by immanence and immanence by transcendence that the two appear as opposites, cancelling each other out without remainder. But this will not do. It will be much more helpful if transcendence and immanence could be seen as mutually enriching concepts rather than mutually destructive. And I suggest that if we opt for the model of the world as God's body, it turns out that we are able to provide a better account not only of immanence but even of transcendence than we could do on the model of cosmic dualism.

The doctrine of transcendence, after all, can hardly fail to generate enormous problems for theology quite apart from the difficulty of reconciling it with a doctrine of immanence. This can be seen by reference to some words of Thomas Aquinas and the teaching of the Church based upon it. Thomas once wrote categorically: 'In this way . . . God and prime matter are distinguished: one is pure act, the other is pure potency, and they agree in nothing.'[1] Now 'prime matter' for Aquinas was a technical term of Aristotelian origins whose meaning we will shortly explore; it did not simply mean the created universe. Nevertheless God and the universe are sharply contrasted: in so far as the latter is material, it is utterly other than God. Indeed, it has been cogently argued that the whole of Aquinas's theology is directly dependent upon the axiom that God is pure act and hence upon his essential difference from the world.[2] This theological position has dominated orthodoxy: in the documents of the First Vatican Council, for example, we find the following:

> The Holy, Catholic, Apostolic, Roman Church believes and confesses that there is one true and living God, Creator and Lord of Heaven and earth, almighty, eternal, immense, incomprehensible, infinite in intelligence, in will, and in all perfection, who, as being one, sole, absolutely simple and immutable spiritual substance, is to be declared really and essentially distinct from the world, of supreme beatitude in and from himself, and ineffably exalted above all things beside himself which exist or are conceivable.[3]

But if the transcendence of God is interpreted, as it seems to be here, as essential distinction from the world, if God and matter agree in *nothing*, then nothing material could, *qua* material, be in any sense revelatory of God. But this means that we have a split between God and the world of such magnitude that we could not learn anything about the nature of God from the nature of the world. God could only be described in contrast to the material universe; and since our language is rooted in our natural environment, this means that we will be able to speak of God only by way

1. Thomas Aquinas *Summa Contra Gentiles* I. 17.7.
2. R. Garrigou-Lagrange *God: His Existence and Nature: A Thomistic Solution of Certain Agnostic Antinomies.*
3. *The Decrees of the Vatican Council.* ed. V. McNabb.

of negative abstractions. However, if this is so, then we have no positive knowledge of God whatsoever, not even the knowledge of whether or not he is worthy of worship, since he might equally be not-strong as not-weak, not-good as not-evil. Any selection among negative abstractions requires some positive criterion upon whose basis such selection can be made, but if there were *no* knowledge obtainable through nature, then such a criterion would not be forthcoming.

This epistemological consequence of such a strong version of divine transcendence is not always adequately recognized, either by those following in the footsteps of Thomas Aquinas or by those Protestant theologians like Karl Barth who in his early writings stresses the total otherness of God. For it is important to notice that, whatever Barth might say to the contrary, an appeal to revelation could not help us here. For if divine transcendence is interpreted as complete otherness, total contrast with the world, then nothing revelatory could in principle occur *within* the natural order, since it is by definition utterly different from God and hence could not reveal him. But if something revelatory were to occur *outside* the world (whatever that might mean), humans could not know it as long as they belong to the world. The only alternative, barring a revision of the concept of transcendence, would be to assert, as Plotinus did, that the soul is *also* utterly other than matter, so that it can obtain knowledge of God not from any consideration of the world and its events, but by elevation to direct mystical communion. But Christian theology since Athanasius – even Christian mystical theology – has firmly rejected this view, finding the significant cleavage not between material substance and spiritual substance as Plotinus did but between the created and the uncreated. Even when it is held that man is a complex of body and soul, it is not a question of God and the soul standing together over against an alien physical universe, but rather of the human person, part of the universe, trying to come to knowledge of and communion with a transcendent God. If transcendence is defined as utter difference, this would seem to be impossible.

Furthermore, as we saw in the previous chapter, such a view would make it difficult to account for any interaction between God and the world. How could a God who was totally and utterly other than the world and anything in it manifest himself in the sacraments, 'fruit of the vine and work of human hands'? What interpretation could conceivably be given to those seminal words, 'And the Word became flesh and dwelt among us, and we beheld his glory . . .'? Not even a weak view of incarnation – that is, one which holds only that Jesus of Nazareth was a man who more clearly than other human beings showed what God is like – would be possible, for if God is utterly other, then he is not *like* anything or anyone, including Jesus. Supernatural reality, on this view,

. . . is precisely what nature is not, and therefore its relations with nature are necessarily problematic, just as Descartes found it impossible to reach a satisfactory understanding of the relation between mind and matter precisely because he had begun by defining them in opposition to one another. In particular, any historical activity of God will tend to take the form of an isolated intervention which is also a violation of the natural.[4]

But it ought certainly to be objected that this is a caricature of the doctrine of transcendence as used by both Catholic and Protestant theologians. For whatever is meant by transcendence, it cannot mean such utter difference that the doctrine of man as created 'in the image and likeness of God' is lost. Many theologians still retain a Thomistic doctrine of analogy, and as long as that is held, it includes a notion of likeness between God and man: whatever the Vatican Council said about the utter distinctness between God and the world, we cannot be interpreting it rightly if we take them to be ruling out the possibility of analogy. And Karl Barth, though in his earlier writings he particularly stresses the otherness of God, later on says:

'In our likeness,' means to be created as a being whose nature is decisively characterized by the fact that although it is created by God it is not a new nature to the extent that it has a pattern in the nature of God himself . . . It is in the coexistence of God and man on the one hand, and man's independent existence on the other, that the real and yet not discordant counterpart in God himself finds creaturely form and is revealed to the creature.[5]

This then leaves us with the task of giving content to the notion of transcendence. In what sense is God wholly other, utterly distinct, and in what sense is there a likeness between God and man? If the doctrine is an important one, we can hardly be content to leave it in this 'neti, neti' state. Rather, our motivation is strengthened for a reassessment of the doctrine of transcendence. And yet such a

4. Colin Gunton *Becoming and Being: The Doctrine of God in Charles Hartshorne and Karl Barth* p. 2.
5. Karl Barth *Church Dogmatics* III. 1 pp. 183–4; cf. his *The Humanity of God*.

programme might well appear dubious. For, whatever interpretation we give it, how could it be adequate if the result is to limit God, to think of him as less than infinite? Yet will not any attempt at thinking of God and the world as one reality not have such limitation as an inevitable consequence? This dilemma, however, is not as impossible to resolve as it at first appears, provided we pay careful attention to several of its key terms.

1. Limitation

The first term to analyse is 'limitation' – a notoriously tricky notion which carries a weight of bogus connotations. It is easy to think of 'limitation' as an evaluative word – that a limited being is somehow not as good as an unlimited one – so that to suggest that God is limited is to say something derogatory about him. But in fact, 'limitation' by itself is evaluatively neutral. Limitation of armaments, for instance, would be very good, and a healthy personal discipline requires many sorts of self-imposed limitations. Indeed, often things which need to be limited are things which in themselves are good: the Greek maxim 'Nothing in excess' could apply only to things which are good or neutral, since in the case of anything intrinsically bad, *any* amount would be too much. 'Limitation' is not a dirty word; neither the entity limited nor the person who limits him- or herself is inferior to the limitless.

'Limitation', therefore, cannot stand by itself. To say that God is unlimited could as easily be to insult him as to praise him: the crucial question is in what *respect* he is limited or unlimited. If we had to say that he was limited in wisdom or goodness, that would be a serious matter indeed for Christian theology, but there are other sorts of limitation which many orthodox theologians have attributed to God. For instance, if there is genuine human freedom, then God is limited (even if it is a self-imposed limitation) in the extent to which he can interfere in human decisions and actions. Again, if God is rational in a sense at all analogous to human rationality, then he is limited by the laws of logic – he cannot rationally contradict himself. Now, if God is not incorporeal, then he is indeed limited by whatever body he has. But whether or not such limitation is theologically acceptable cannot be decided until we know what *sort* of body, and hence what sort of limitation, we are talking about: the mere imputation of the term 'limited' cannot settle the case as we might at first have thought.

We can see this more clearly if we consider various alternatives.

If God is embodied, he is in some respects limited, and the limitation is related to the sort of body he has. But it would be mistaken to suppose that being disembodied would be complete freedom from limitation. An incorporeal being, for instance, would be limited to those sorts of activity which do not require a body for their performance: he could not climb trees, sniff roses, or embrace friends. Embodiment would be a different sort of limitation from disembodiment, and the question is whether it would be a more or less theologically acceptable sort. We ought not to give way to the temptation to believe that embodiment would be a limitation and incorporeality would not.

Now, the limitation with which embodiment confronts us is a spatial limitation, and it might be thought that just this is what is incompatible with a proper understanding of God. Even if we grant that we cannot just say 'God is unlimited', it would not do to think that his limitation is spatial. This, however, has the curious result that, rather than God not having any body at all, his body should be infinitely big: it would amount to deciding on theological grounds the scientific question of whether or not the universe is infinite! However the religious motivation for insisting that God cannot be spatially limited has nothing to do with the size of the universe, but rather with the concern that such a God could not be omnipresent. He could at best be a God after the order of Zeus, powerful and clever, but not omnipotent or omniscient because he is spatially confined. Our considerations of omnipresence in the previous chapter, however, have already dissipated this concern. Omnipresence is not a question of spatial permeation but of omnipotence and omniscience, and since, in the case of God, knowledge and action are always direct, without mediation, these can be better understood on the model of the world as God's body than on a cosmic dualist model. If the universe is God's body, then, if the universe is not spatially infinite, God is not spatially infinite, but this does not affect the doctrine of omnipresence.

Nor would spatial limitation of God be a limitation of his power. His control over the universe would be jeopardized only if the shape and size of the universe and the items within it, and their behaviour, were fixed independently of God. But a theist claims that this is not so. All that exists does so – and does so in the form that it exists, with its own 'natural' laws – by the will of God: thus God could change the shape and contents of the universe in any way he chose. Theists have traditionally held that the world as it is is sustained by the will of God: it is by his grace (not because of the independent stability of the universe) that we are not consumed.

It is worth noticing that this shows again how the analogy of the world as God's body must be qualified. The shape and size of our bodies are largely not in our control: we may, by effort or carelessness, lose or gain a stone or two, but we cannot by taking thought add a cubit to our stature or develop an extra pair of limbs. There is a givenness about what our bodies are like and how they operate. But if what I am suggesting about the relationship of God to the universe is correct, then he can, if he chooses, change his shape and size (we might reflect whimsically that if some 'Big Bang' theory of the origin of the present universe is right, then he has in fact done so). But this qualification, like others we have noted, points again towards more complete embodiment than our own, in the sense that God has a choice about how he is embodied (what his shape and size is to be and how his body is to function) to a far greater extent than we do.

2. Infinity

The notion of infinity is a far more tricky one than that of limitation, in spite of the fact that it is standard theological vocabulary. Grammatically it is not a positive term but a negative one, though it is undeniable that in religious thought and speech it has often been burdened with positive evaluative weight. Its obvious sense is not-finite, and as long as we are sticking to this surface meaning it could not legitimately be used as an expression of merit unless finitude automatically expresses demerit. But why should we assume that it does?

As soon as we attempt to answer this question we come to deeper meanings of 'finite' and 'infinite'. Finitude, like limitation, must always be qualified; it leads to the question 'in what respect?' Things or persons can be finite with respect to duration or size or extent, for instance, or the word can be stretched to apply to concepts like power, goodness, and even life itself. It is curious to notice how infrequently the term is used in the Bible, and the variation of the contexts where it does appear: one of Job's comforters speaks of the wickedness and iniquities of the sufferer as infinite, the strength of a (fallen!) city is described as infinite, and on a more positive note, God's understanding is infinite.[6] But now we are back to the same

6. Job 22:5; Nahum 3:9; Psalm 147:5.

considerations which arose with reference to limitation. *Spatial* finitude would be simply spatial limitation; this is just a part of what we normally mean by having a body and is not an argument for or against having one. The real question, again, is whether embodiment would be a theologically objectionable form of finitude or limitation – whether it would limit God's power, wisdom, goodness, and so on – not whether it would be *any* form of limitation. Unless this is answered affirmatively, there is no reason to argue that God could not be embodied solely on the ground that he would not then be infinite. Although he would not be infinite with respect to physical volume (unless the universe is) this by itself hardly seems theologically significant. But although we might well agree that sheer physical size is not a matter of theological importance, the notion of infinity is often loaded with positive meaning of very great significance which must also be investigated in connection with a model of divine embodiment. This will become clearer in the following sections.

3. Perfection

When a religious person says that God is infinite, part of his or her positive meaning is that God is perfect. This has been given classical formulation by Thomas Aquinas, who explicitly connects ideas of perfection with the doctrine of divine incorporeality in an argument closely related to the idea of God as pure act which we have already discussed. Aquinas says:

> . . . Primordial matter is the most imperfect of all things. For matter as such is only potential, and primordial matter is therefore sheer potentiality and entirely imperfect. We however hold God to be not primordial matter but the primary operative cause of things, and thus the most perfect of things. For just as matter as such is potential, so an acting thing as such is actual. Thus the first origin of all activity will be the most actual, and therefore the most perfect, of all things. For things are called perfect when they have achieved actuality, the perfect being that in which nothing required by the thing's particular mode of perfection fails to exist.[7]

There is no doubt that when people speak of God as infinite, the connotation of his perfection is not far from their minds – this

7. Thomas Aquinas *Summa Theologiae* I. a. 4. 1.

is far more significant than astronomical ideas about unlimited magnitude. And when we think of perfection, especially when we ascribe perfection to God, we normally mean it in a moral sense: thus to say that God is perfect means that he is holy, sinless, pure, and the like. For *us* to strive for perfection (especially as that notion is used in ascetical theology) means to strive to make those attributes of God our own, assisted by divine grace. Now although we shall see that this evaluative sense of perfection provides the motivation lurking behind the Thomistic argument, this is not the primary sense in which he is using the word. The central meaning as Thomas is using 'perfection' is 'complete' or 'total'. In this way it connects with the idea of infinity, since the infinite is by definition partial rather than total. In itself, this idea of infinity or perfection need have no evaluative connotation: we could describe someone as a perfectly good person, but we can also speak of a perfect fool, a perfect nuisance, and a perfect circle. As Thomas himself commented just prior to the argument already quoted, perfect, 'etymologically . . . means "thoroughly made".'

This notion of perfection as 'thoroughness' or 'completeness' – we might call it a metaphysical rather than a moral notion – is the peg on which the argument hangs. Aquinas, along with other theologians who are unwilling to ascribe any change or development to God, says that God is already perfect, complete, and hence changeless because it is incoherent to think of a perfect being developing and becoming more perfect. The important point here is that Thomas believes he can make his case without any further qualifications simply by contrasting God with matter: a material object could not in principle be metaphysically complete, while an incorporeal one could. But why should he think so? What leads Aquinas to the belief that incorporeality is intrinsically connected with metaphysical perfection – that is, why would God's *not* having a body make him complete in a way which he would not be if he had one?

Until we begin to move within the Thomistic metaphysical circle of actuality and potentiality, we may well have thought that the opposite conclusion was more probable – that if God does not have a body, then there is something which he lacks, and though this lack might not be important for religious purposes, he would not be complete or perfect in the Thomistic sense. But as we saw earlier, according to Aquinas God is *actus purus,* with no potentiality. He is the First Cause, the one who forms all things and is himself formed by none. To be 'most actual', therefore, is synonymous with being perfect, complete. There is nothing which remains incomplete or merely potential in God, since God is himself the origin of all that is actual. Aquinas's 'proof' of God's perfection, therefore, is not so much a proof as a corollary: once it has been granted that God is the First Cause, his immateriality, actuality, immutability, and perfection are all implied and can be derived just by thinking out the meanings of the terms.

It is a tightly woven web; but we have already seen how extensively it unravels when we pull at the threads of immutability and actuality. I wish now to suggest that, when we give a similar tug to the thread of perfection, the fabric disintegrates completely, and the whole thing turns out to be a version of the Emperor's New Clothes. As we saw, Aquinas is not using the term 'perfection' in an explicitly moral sense in his argument, but rather in the sense of completeness, '. . . the perfect thing being that in which nothing required by the thing's particular mode of perfection fails to exist'. But as it stands, that is not very informative. As we have already seen in the case of words like 'unlimited' and 'infinite', so here too we are forced to ask, perfect in what *respect*? If 'perfect' simply means 'complete', we can hardly just say that God is perfect in every respect: no one is willing to say that God is a perfect fool, a perfect bore or a perfect circle! So if we are going to say that God is perfect, we have to be able to specify in what respect this perfection is meant.

Aquinas is of course aware of this, and has already spoken of the *mode* of a thing's perfection; thus only the sorts of perfection appropriate to God are to be predicated of him. But this does not get us very much further. We feel instinctively that foolishness, boredom and circularity are not appropriate to God, and that wisdom and goodness are. But what are the criteria of appropriateness which we might use to decide a questionable case – in particular, how are we to decide whether embodiment is or is not appropriate for divine completeness? Simple appeal to metaphysical perfection cannot settle this question: after all, it is open to anyone to argue that God is perfectly (that is, completely) embodied. Although this is clearly not what Aquinas intended, within the terms of his argument as set forth to this point it would be a legitimate move.

I suggested earlier that Thomas's argument is closer to ordinary religious ideas of perfection than might at first be evident. This becomes manifest when we see that, even though the primary use of 'perfection' in his argument is metaphysical, an evaluative sense is also near at hand. We can infer from the *sed contra* of the article that it was not far from his mind. It is taken from the Gospel of Matthew: 'be ye perfect, as your heavenly Father is perfect.' If we suppose that the line of his argument is entirely metaphysical, this is a very curious prefix to use as the beginning of his reply. After all, his train of thought from *actus purus* to perfection is such that, if this is the notion of perfection employed by the writer of Scripture, Jesus was demanding the impossible – even the ridiculous: how could Jesus tell men to become perfect if perfection involves being pure act and incorporeal? A moral ideal of perfection, even if it is unattainable, at least provides us with a direction for our striving, but it is nonsense to set about striving to become pure act. The Gospel writer could hardly have thought that Jesus intended us to strive towards perfection in this sense, or that these words contained any hidden implication that God is incorporeal. And surely Thomas, also, was well aware of that.

But then why did he quote this verse at the opening of the argument? What is its role in his train of thought? The command to be perfect in the words ascribed to Jesus is quite clearly a moral command; an injunction, in the context, to be more charitable than the 'publicans', who do good only to those from whom they think they may expect good in return. Such goodness is contrasted with the goodness of God, who 'makes his sun rise on good and bad alike, and sends rain on the honest and the dishonest', and who is thus the model for us to follow in learning to obey Jesus' injunction to love and do good even to our enemies: we are to be perfect just as he is perfect. It might plausibly be suggested that the exhortation to perfection refers to more than the passage immediately preceding it, and is a summary and encapsulation of the whole sermon. But the teaching throughout the sermon, as in the immediate context of the quotation, is moral, not metaphysical. It does not on the face of it have anything to do with the doctrine of divine incorporeality, let alone suggest that we should strive towards incorporeality too!

But for Aquinas the case was more complex. Moral perfection, here enjoined upon us by the example of our heavenly Father, was linked, in his view, with the metaphysical perfection of God. This follows from his belief, which he derived from the tradition of Plato, Plotinus and Augustine, that Goodness and Being are ultimately identical. He explicitly argues for this identification in the very next question of the *Summa:* the essence of goodness consists in its desirability, and a thing is desirable only in so far as it is perfect:

111

And the perfection of a thing depends on how far it has achieved actuality. It is clear then that a thing is good insomuch as it exists . . . Obviously then being good does not really differ from existing.[8]

The monumental significance of this position and its extended influence in theology can hardly be overestimated. In this context, however, I must limit myself to a few comments on the double sense in which the word 'perfection' is used, which links it with both actuality and goodness and contrasts it with matter, so that a being who is both morally and metaphysically perfect must also be incorporeal.

In the first place, if Aquinas means to stick by his definition of perfection as completeness, he needs this further argument to link up perfection and goodness, otherwise why should we think that there can be no such thing as a perfect devil? Unless he introduces an explicitly *moral* aspect of perfection, the simple assertion of perfection guarantees nothing about the moral quality of the subject. Yet the argument which he uses to show the identification of perfection and goodness is highly debatable. It is by no means obvious that the goodness of a thing consists in its being desirable: this raises the question of 'desirable to whom?' If the answer is 'to everyone', then the conclusion does not follow, since some people desire evil things. If, however, the answer is 'to good people', then we are left with the question of how these are to be identified, and it will be hard to escape the circle generated by defining good people as those who desire good things. But even if this problem is overlooked, further hurdles lie ahead. If desirability is consequent upon perfection, then the moral connotation of 'perfection' has already been smuggled in, since desirability is *not* consequent upon perfection understood simply as completeness: the more 'perfectly' a perfect devil is perfect, the less desirable he is! If this moral connotation has already been introduced, then the argument begs the question, since it assumes the identity of completeness and goodness rather than proves it. Thus either the argument is circular, or else it rests upon the false premise that desirability is consequent merely upon completeness.

Suppose, however, that in spite of this we accepted the Thomistic conclusion, and agreed that the infinite is the perfect, morally and metaphysically, and that metaphysical completeness requires incorporeality: what would be the implications of such a conclusion? An

8. Ibid., 5. 1.

immediate result of this chain of implications would be that only the incorporeal can be unqualifiedly good. If the infinite is the perfect, in the moral as well as the metaphysical sense, then any embodied being must be less than perfect. Apart from its ramifications for the doctrine of the incarnation, this verdict might be accepted, especially by those who take seriously the contrast between the infinite perfection of God and the finitude and sinfulness of humankind. H.P. Owen, for example, writes:

All human behaviour approaches perfection to the extent that it expresses wisdom, goodness, and love. Yet although the body aids these spiritual properties insofar as it offers a medium for their expression, it also inhibits them in many – and some tragically frustrating – ways. Hence only pure Spirit can constitute an absolutely perfect form of personal existence.[9]

However, we have already seen that divine knowledge and action can be understood better if we consider the world as God's body than if we think of God as pure Spirit, and that such moral infirmities as are occasioned by our embodiment (as opposed to weakness or badness of wills) would be diminished, not by becoming incorporeal, but by what I have described as more complete embodiment. If the whole universe is the body of God, then, unlike human persons whose bodies and actions are restricted, God has unlimited immediate knowledge and all his actions are basic actions, not inhibited in the ways that ours are.

But a more serious implication follows from the Thomistic triad. If the incorporeal is the most real and the most good, then the corporeal, matter, is the least real and the least good. Now, this negative view of matter is not a novelty introduced by Aquinas; as we shall soon see, it had a long tenure in theological metaphysics before and after his time. And its point for us is that, if incorporeality is identified with goodness, then matter – and physical bodies in so far as they are material – must be identified with evil. If God is defined as totally other than the material world, then the world is totally other than God: the universe is desacralized, and God no longer has any part in it. The moral and religious consequences of this are enormous: sin and evil are inherently connected with the body (and often specifically with sexuality), so that persons must fight against their physicality as alien to the spirit, thus producing a split in human wholeness in the name of religion – these evils

9. H.P. Owen *Concepts of Deity* p. 28.

of false asceticism have been frequently noticed in recent year:
Furthermore, what has often escaped attention is that, if God
separated off from the material world, then all exploration of the
world can have nothing to do with God. Nor can it have anythin
to do with goodness. It is utterly secular and at best amoral. T
the extent that there is a schism between science and technolog
on the one hand and religion and ethics on the other, part
the responsibility must rest on those who, by identifying God ar
goodness with the immaterial, have banished them from the wor
in which we live. Descartes, in his contribution to the desacraliz
tion of the universe, could have appealed to Thomistic theology
an ally in this respect.

Of course Thomists and others who accept the position of classic
theism on this point will insist that these consequences can
mitigated by a balancing emphasis on divine immanence and t
doctrines of creation and providence. But if the triad of identificati
of reality, goodness and incorporeality is taken seriously, then
appeal to divine immanence in (evil) matter is difficult to susta.
It begins to look more and more like what its proponents wou d
call a mystery and everyone else would call a contradiction. T s
is a harsh judgement, and, I admit, a hasty one: it will rece e
more warrant through the discussion of the concepts of matter a d
transcendence.

4. Matter

It is not only charitable, it is philosophically profitable to exam e
why Aquinas made the triadic identification as he did. It is a o
worth while to see in more detail why thinkers in this century, b h
scientists and theologians, find it unacceptable. Both these aims n
be achieved by a brief excursion into the concept of matter a
concept that has been central to a whole series of philosoph al
systems from Anaximenes to Karl Marx, and the content of wl h
has changed radically in the 2500 years of its history. The cen al
ingredients in the idea of matter as used in classical theism are as
we have seen, that matter is least real, least good, and least inte g-
ible; and these ideas can be better understood if their lineag is
known at least in outline, and better overcome if we catch ev a
brief glimpse of the contrasting attitudes of modern science.

The Greek word for matter is ὕλη, and apparently m nt
'timber'.[10] It denoted the anchor in the sea of change: if there o

10. Cf. Ernan McMullin, ed., *The Concept of Matter in Greek and Medieval Philosop*.

114

be genuine change, real newness, then there must be something that changes, and this underlying substratum is matter. But if matter is that which supports change, and if change is to be understood as a succession of properties or qualities, then matter, the substratum underlying these changes, cannot itself have properties. It is susceptible to any form whatever, and therefore it can have no special form of its own. Accordingly, a body, whether of an inanimate object or a living thing, is not simply matter but a union of matter and form.

There was, to be sure, considerable difference between Plato and Aristotle on the meaning of 'form' and on its nature and origin. But there was less difference in their concept of matter. Both thought of it as the substratum which of itself was 'nothing', and became something only by being formed, thus receiving qualities. Consequently matter as such, mutability *per se*, is unintelligible: it is not knowable because of itself it has no qualities or properties which are the means by which we intellectually grasp things. Forms are thus the bearers of intelligibility and the imparters of reality; matter in itself is 'nearly nothing', as Plotinus was to put it.[11] Thus one ascends the hierarchy of rationality and reality in direct proportion as one moves away from bare matter in the 'great chain of being'. Since the Platonic system also identified reality and goodness (the Form of the Good is the ultimate form, and has 'most being'), matter in that system is also least good. It is true enough that Christianity in its development allied itself more closely with Neoplatonism, which saw matter as imperfect but ultimately derived from the One/Good, than with Manichaeism, which saw matter as an autonomous principle of evil, decay and corruption. Yet no less a figure than Augustine of Hippo thought that, in original sin, matter and the fall were interlinked, and therefore spiritual warfare was a warfare against matter, which could be described *inter alia* as passion, unreason, inertia, or man's lower nature. (The popular identification of 'sex' and 'sin' has a long history!) At best, matter could be transformed, raised up; often however theologians spoke instead of transcending it, obliterating it, or escaping from it.

As a matter of fact, Thomas Aquinas was not as sharp a dualist as many who had come before him. Matter is not accidental to his system; it is the principle of individuation, as it had been for Aristotle. Items of our experience do not usually have absolutely unique characteristics; animals and plants, for instance, can be divided into

11. Plotinus *Enneads* II. 4. 16: cf. III. 6. 13.

species, with members of the same species sharing family resemblances with one another. We are able to group them together on the basis of these shared characteristics which we conceptualize, so that we label one group 'bluebell', another 'redwood', and another 'meadow lark'. The properties which are constitutive of anything which would fall under these concepts Aquinas calls its form, thus staying roughly within the Aristotelian tradition.[12] For example, yellow and black throat markings and a distinctive trill are aspects of the form of meadow lark; they are two of its distinctive characteristics. But forms by themselves do not exist. There is no such thing in the world as meadowlarkhood, there are only individual meadow larks – this one, sitting on this fence post singing, that one, with its feathers fluffed out against the chilling rain. So individual things must be more than forms; they are a unit of existence comprising both form and matter.

It is well to note that 'matter' here is being used in a technical sense, consonant with the Aristotelian tradition, and some distance from the modern sense in which an apple or a human body is material. It is the underlying substance which individuates things once they are formed, and which otherwise has no existence of its own but is pure passive potentiality. Clearly if matter is defined in this technical sense then God cannot be material, since matter is pure passivity – but then, neither can people, plants, or even stones, all of which are actual. It is a very long jump from saying that God cannot be material in this technical sense of matter to saying that he cannot be embodied, and many of the difficulties theologians might raise in speaking of an embodied God have their roots, I suggest, in a failure to observe the difference.

With the possible exception of the Stoics, the view of matter as the inert substratum underlying change and in itself passive dominated thought about physical objects (and corresponded with the postulation of an activating immaterial soul) throughout the formative period of classical theological metaphysics. However, post-Newtonian and especially post-Einsteinian science has developed quite a different idea of what matter is, culminating in the discovery of the interconvertibility of matter and energy and verified, for good or ill, in the splitting of the atom and the development of nuclear energy. From this perspective one can hardly continue to speak of matter as pure inert potentiality, sitting pudding-like waiting to be

12. Cf. John Goheen *The Problem of Matter and Form in De Ente et Essentia of Thomas Aquinas*.

acted upon. It is even questionable whether we can speak of matter at all, as such, or whether in the end we must substitute talk about force-fields and patterns of energy.

Theologians cannot be content to ignore such major shifts in scientific perspective. Nevertheless it would be too hasty to move at once to a denial of the potentiality of matter. For although modern science cannot accept the view that matter is utterly inert, requiring something incorporeal to give it form and energize it, it may still be true that mass-energy has no self-direction. Although there is motion and energy, there is no goal, no formative or purpose activity in all the expenditure of energy, and for this a non-material rational agent is necessary. Atoms of aluminium, iron, and other metals will never form themselves into a space ship: as far as any purposive activity is concerned mass-energy, for all its force-fields and motion, is just the pure potentiality which Aquinas considered it to be, and as much in need of a rational agent to order it and direct it. And since matter in this sense is pure potentiality, the rational agent must be the opposite: *qua* rational the agent must be immaterial.

But this will not do. It makes considerable sense to think of matter as pure potentiality as long as we think in terms of lumps of metal, sand, stones, or candle wax: all of these need external agents to act upon them if they are to be fashioned to fulfil a human purpose. But quite apart from the blatant anthropocentricity of this perspective, it has an enormous objection to overcome. These sorts of things are not, after all, the only or even the most significant items of our acquaintance. How is the argument affected if we pass from inanimate objects to living things – plants, animals, and even ourselves? Here, it seems, we have two alternatives: either we can say that animate material differs from inanimate in that, at least at this level (whatever must be said about its sub-atomic components) it is self-directing and active and not pure potentiality. Or we can say that the *matter* of living things is as thoroughly in potentiality as the matter of sand and coal dust, but that it is activated by an incorporeal mind or soul.

An influential variety of the latter course was taken by Aristotle, for instance, who posited a variety of souls which inform matter, thus making things to be what they are: the nutritive soul is the principle of plant life, the sensitive soul that of animal life, and the rational soul informs human beings. In Aristotle, however, the coalition of form and matter was not seen as the coming together of two discrete entities, a soul and a physical body, which could each exist separately. As we have already seen, he did not think there was any unformed matter, nor (unlike Plato) that there were any immaterial souls waiting for prospective bodies. The living plant, he held, just *is* an organism characterized by matter seeking its own nourishment and thus producing fruit. Thomas Aquinas, while closely following Aristotle in many respects, modified his tone in a Platonic–Augustinian direction. He said, for instance, that living things are moved *by* their souls; and although he was adamant that the soul of a man is not a man, nevertheless he did believe that the soul could exist without the body while awaiting the body's resurrection at the last day.

But the really fascinating case for our purposes is Descartes, who absorbed the ancient and medieval teaching on souls and body and refashioned it in a more secular manner, forming a pivot point between ancient and modern thought. Descartes believed that matter in itself operates on strictly mechanical principles (and hence that animals are automata, activated like clocks, since they do not have souls) but that in the case of human beings, the material body is somehow inhabited by a soul, the essence of which is rationality. The soul of a person could exist without a body; indeed, the soul is the real person. For a strict Cartesian it would be a contradiction in terms to speak of living matter: only souls can truly be said to be alive. We speak loosely when we speak of living bodies; if we were accurate we would have to say that a material body cannot as such be alive, but that it can somehow be inhabited and activated by a living soul. The all-absorbing philosophical task then becomes the effort to explain how this could be possible.

The impact of this Cartesian split between mind and matter has been felt in science and philosophy ever since. Herbert Feigl usefully contrasts the post-Cartesian concepts of matter and mind as follows:[13]

Mental	*Physical*
subjective (private)	objective (public)
nonspatial	spatial
qualitative	quantitative
purposive	mechanical
mnemic	non-mnemic
holistic	atomistic
emergent	compositional
intentional	'blind'; nonintentional

13. Herbert Feigl *The 'Mental' and the 'Physical'* p. 29.

This contrast also shows that the material world must be held to operate according to relatively simple mechanical laws, which also apply to the human body. The paradigm structure is a piece of clockwork, whose functions are explicable by reference to causal interaction of a mechanical sort. The task of the physiologist is to show the extent to which the human body is also a mechanism, and to display its interacting laws. Human behaviour which cannot be explained in this way is the result of the soul, and is inexplicable, because it is not amenable to mechanical causal systems. Even so critical a thinker as Kant, in discussing alternatives proposed to give account of apparent purposiveness in the universe, maintains a roughly Cartesian contrast between the mental and the physical. He says:

> The possibility of living matter is quite inconceivable. The very conception of it involves self-contradiction, since lifelessness, *inertia*, constitutes the essential characteristic of matter.[14]

Now, if this perspective is accepted, then obviously matter is indeed potentiality in the relevant sense and can only be acted on in any purposive way by something non-material. Thus God, as primary activator, would have to be pure spirit. But must we adopt it? The other (roughly Aristotelian) perspective, that human and animal bodies and even plants are genuinely alive, living matter, not just inert matter inhabited by living souls, is much more congenial to modern biological trends. In this view there could be growth and development, and, at higher levels, self-direction and intentional agency and consciousness, in a way which the Platonic–Cartesian view would find difficult to account for. Indeed, it sounds quaint to our post-Darwinian ears to hear talk of souls using our bodies to get from place to place or to accomplish our activities, as though bodies were a kind of lorry for the transportation of souls.

However, custom is no sure guide to truth, and we must shortly look further at the issues involved. But this much has already emerged. If a strict form of dualism is true, that is, if it is true that persons are composed of incorporeal souls acting upon physical mechanical bodies, then we can say that matter is potentiality and God must be incorporeal. But if it is false, and we can speak with biologists of genuinely living matter, then matter is not necessarily pure potentiality: the matter that composes a living human body, at least, would have to be described in some other way.

14. Immanuel Kant *Critique of Judgment* II.12.

As early as the seventeenth century, doubts began to arise about Descartes' description of matter as essentially unthinking extended mechanical clockwork. Spinoza, for instance, rejected Descartes' dualistic system in favour of a holistic approach in which rationality and extension are attributes of a single substance. Considering the objection that this would make matter capable of far more than could be allowed for on simple mechanistic operation, Spinoza says:

> No one has hitherto laid down the limits to the powers of the body, that is, no one has yet been taught by experience what the body can accomplish solely by the laws of nature, in so far as she is regarded as extension.[15]

After all, Spinoza points out, people do remarkable things in their sleep, which, on a Cartesian theory, would have to be imputed to the physical mechanism alone, the mind being dormant. If matter can do things like that, why set limits in advance as to its other possibilities? The boundary between what matter can and cannot do should not be stipulated *a priori*.

Locke went further. Although he, like Descartes, was a dualist, he was sharply critical of aspects of the Cartesian position. In particular, Locke wondered aloud about any *a priori* restrictions on the abilities of matter. Even if matter is on the whole the inert substance which Descartes had described (and which Locke reaffirmed) it requires no more effort to imagine God giving matter the power to think than it does to imagine God conjoining minds and bodies – but dualists believe that he regularly does the latter. Locke comments:

> it being, in respect of our notions, not much more remote from our comprehension to conceive, that God can, if he pleases, superadd to matter a faculty of thinking, than that he should superadd to it another substance, with a faculty of thinking; since we know not wherein thinking consists, nor to what sort of substances the Almighty has been pleased to give that power.[16]

Locke emphasizes that he is only speculating, and that it is not because he really believes that matter can think but rather because he believes that philosophers should keep within the constraints of modesty that he complains about the dogmatism of Cartesians. However, the materialists of the French Enlightenment, men like

15. Spinoza *Ethics* III. II Note.
16. John Locke *An Essay Concerning Human Understanding* IV. III. 6.

La Mettrie and the Baron d'Holbach, took up seriously this idea of thinking matter – a contradiction in terms on the Cartesian system – and protested that at the very least it was grave presumption to assume that there could be no distinction between *kinds* of matter, or to suppose that all matter is in its very nature inert.

Post-Enlightenment science has, on the whole, sided against Descartes. Physicists now would reject his ideas of clockwork mechanism as fantastically simplistic, and the notion that matter is inert and needs a push from outside to get it going has long since been obsolete. Even more significant than developments in physics is the growth of the life sciences, especially biology and physiology, which have begun to recognize the enormous (and unmechanical) structure and ability of the human brain. Indeed it is part of this recognition that makes it increasingly problematic to think of human persons on the old dualist model of a body-piece and a soul-piece: at least, this model would have to be revised in such a way that it could take account of the developing understanding of living bodies. Now, as we have seen, the doctrine of divine incorporeality would be a consequence only of the view that matter is pure potentiality. But this idea in turn is persuasive only so long as we think in terms of inanimate lumps of stuff: when we turn our attention to living things we are far less likely to accept such an account of matter. But if it is the case that there is genuinely living matter, human bodies, for instance, then whatever other reasons there might have been for saying that God is spirit, we could not object to the suggestion that the world is his body solely on the grounds that bodies are material and matter is pure potentiality, for we have already granted that human beings themselves are an exception to such a view. And if the world is to furnish us with any models of the divine nature at all, human beings are the most likely choice.

With this sketch of the history of the concept of matter, we can see more clearly why, given the philosophical framework of their times, theologians like Thomas Aquinas would see matter as least real, least good, and least intelligible. We can also see, however, that such a view of matter does not have the support of modern science. It would be very difficult to defend, nowadays, the view that matter is unreal or even least real in the sense that Aquinas thought it was, that it is a mere receptacle for intelligible forms. The question then arises about the relationship between reality and goodness. If the identity is retained, we must say that matter, since it is real, is good. If it is not retained, then matter is evaluatively neutral. Whichever alternative is taken, it is clear that the triad of moral perfection, metaphysical reality, and incorporeality is broken. If the real is the good, then given the reality of matter a corporeal being would not be less good than an incorporeal one just because it was embodied. If the real is morally neutral, then so is matter, and again incorporeality could not be preferred on grounds that it was morally better than embodiment. A God embodied in the universe would not, from the point of view of modern understanding of matter, be morally inferior to an incorporeal God.

It is well to take stock of where we are. We began with an account of how a theologically rich notion of infinity might lead one to say that an infinite being must be morally perfect, and that perfection is incompatible with embodiment. But we found that this incompatibility would obtain only if matter were looked upon in a way which is no longer tenable. The idea of matter as utterly alien to us, incapable of thought or life, and hence unworthy to be predicated of God, is a view which theology must follow science in rejecting. The holism and integration of human persons which religion strives for, integration with the world, with other men and women, and with our own bodies, is incompatible with a derogatory evaluation of matter. But this means that, with a more positive view of matter, the way is open to consider its relationship to God, on the model of divine embodiment in the world.

5. Transcendence

We have been discussing the relationship between limitation, infinity and perfection, and have seen that all of these allow for the idea of divine embodiment. But it is time to give a positive account of the doctrine of God's transcendence, to show that it, too, is more congenial to the model of God and the universe as one reality than to the monarchical view. Indeed, considering the universe to be the embodiment of God sheds new light on the doctrine of transcendence and removes some of the problems of its relationship to immanence.

If the universe is thought of in physical terms as consisting of all matter and energy in all its configurations and interrelationships, then if the universe is God's body, God must be composed of matter and energy and must be in a direct physical relationship with the whole universe. Stated in such bald terms, that sounds more like a crass theological joke than like a seriously defensible theological position. It would seem to condemn us to materialism, or at best to some variety of pantheism. I suggest, however, that as we explore it further, its implications will be far more enlightening than at first appears.

However, it does bring out another reason why it would not do to say that God has a body which is only part of the universe in the way that *our* bodies are parts of it. If God had a body like ours, then he would be influenced by – would at a physical level interact with – all other physical things. Gravity, radiation, chemical processes would all somehow affect God in the same ways as they affect other material objects. This would be a startling conclusion for a traditional theist to come to, since it would rule out not only transcendence but also divine omnipotence (because God would then be subject to, rather than master of, forces like gravitation) and indestructibility (what would happen if God ventured too near a black hole?). Nor would it help to suggest that God was a 'superman' – that is, able to escape from natural forces – for although such an expedient might give God power over *some* such forces, it could not be compatible with omnipotence as long as the notion of 'physical body' continued to mean anything like what it ordinarily means. These are crude ways of putting the issues, but their very crudeness shows how our concept of divinity would be seriously undermined by the suggestion that God has a body located somewhere in the universe. This is perhaps one of the worries which prompts theologians to say that God could not be a being among beings, somehow on a level with natural objects: this theme will arise again in the next chapter.

But what about the idea that God is coextensive with the universe? Does this notion fare any better in relation to transcendence? We have already noted that the idea of transcendence is a difficult one; it is another of those terms used regularly and vigorously defended in theological discussion without due attention to its meaning. But how should it be defined? A glance at the dictionary can provide us with raw materials for analysis. The definition given for transcendence is

> of supreme merit or quality, (of God) existing apart from, or not subject to the limitations of, material universe (opp. immanent).

And if, for completeness, we include the definition of immanence, we have

> inherent; (of God) permanently pervading the universe (opp. transcendent).[17]

17. *Oxford English Dictionary.*

123

When we recall that traditional theology wishes to affirm that God is both transcendent and immanent, we naturally feel puzzled. We have already discussed the doctrine of divine perfection and shown that it cannot be simply identified with incorporeality, so we will leave aside the evaluative aspect of these definitions. Transcendence and immanence then appear to be directly contradictory concepts, the former indicating separateness from the universe and the latter claiming that God pervades the universe. And it is too often the case that theologians so qualify the doctrine of immanence by transcendence, and transcendence by immanence, that it would be difficult to say whether anything remains of either. The logical problems are sometimes shrugged off (or even welcomed) as mystery. But surely an account which could illuminate the concepts so that we need not perform these mental gymnastics in the name of 'intellectual good works' would be preferable.

In the previous sections of this chapter, we noted that the phrase 'not subject to limitations' is inadequate, since we are then still bound to ask 'which limitations'. If spatial limitations are meant, then transcendence has been reduced to meaning 'not spatially limited'. But apart from the fact that such a reduction of its meaning does not do justice to the religious significance of transcendence, it has one of two consequences: either it means that God/the universe is infinite in size, thus making a dubious scientific pronouncement from an equally dubious theological platform, or else it is a mere assertion of divine incorporeality rather than an argument for it, and it would remain to show why spatial limitations should be incompatible with deity. If, however, other limitations than spatial ones are meant, then we must ask which ones: what sort of limitations, other than spatial, does embodiment involve, and how are these incompatible with transcendence? But now we are back with the question from which we began; 'Tis plain that we do dance round in a circle.'

We can find a new start by thinking again of our basic model for theological understanding. If God is personal, and human persons are our best available model for an understanding of what God is like, then reconsidering the relationship between personhood and embodiment in human persons may help us to understand how God could be embodied in the universe. This approach is all the more promising because a particular use of transcendence which has attracted considerable attention in recent years is the idea of the transcendence of *persons*. Although we are frail, finite creatures, a part of the world of nature and produced by natural evolutionary

124

processes, reeds within the tidal beds of endless flux, we are still, to use Pascal's phrase, 'thinking reeds'. Personal consciousness, which emerges through physical and biological processes, nevertheless seeks intelligibility and meaning in those very processes, and in that sense transcends them. Human consciousness, human personality, freedom, feelings, and a sense of moral responsibility are not peripheral to the idea of what it means to be personal; yet unless we revert to a Platonic–Cartesian dualism, these aspects of personhood, though they transcend the material world, are rooted in that very physicality which they transcend. Although a person's thoughts are more than his or her brain processes, and human loves and hatreds more than chemical balances, yet if the brain processes and the chemistry were tampered with or obliterated, so also would be the thoughts and feelings. If we can begin to give some sense to the 'more than' phrase, we will be nearer to an understanding of what is involved in transcendence.

This idea of human transcendence, a significant theme in recent continental philosophy, has been turned to theological purpose by Karl Rahner, who in his book *The Foundations of Christian Faith* uses the concept of transcendence of persons as the keystone for his whole theological framework. Human persons, while obviously embodied, are transcendent beings; for Rahner this means beings open to reason, to emotion, to responsibility, and to what he calls 'the mysterious infinity'. The transcendence of a human person is to be found in openness to meaning and reality which comes to the person within the spatio-temporal situation, not somehow apart from it. Yet in spite of the fact that it is *within* the spatio-temporal, it cannot be *reduced* to the spatio-temporal. Thus although Rahner (and others like him) are not content to think of the transcendence of persons as merely an aspect of their souls, unrelated to their physicality, they are equally opposed to reductionism. Although they of course agree that for some purposes biology and physiology are of very great importance, the significance of human thought and action cannot be reduced to a set of physiological data, however complex. The really important consideration in saying that human persons are transcendent is, thus, that they cannot be fully described or understood in strictly physiological or mechanical terms: the opposite of 'transcendent' turns out to be not 'immanent' but 'reducible'. But clearly this does not mean that human persons are disembodied – that the physical and mechanical sorts of description have no place whatever. Obviously they do. But their place must be within the framework of the larger understanding of what it is to be a person; they cannot themselves be that framework.

This idea of the immanence and transcendence of human persons, and the corollary that reductionist accounts of personhood are mistaken, has enormous bearing on the doctrine of the transcendence of God. If human beings cannot be adequately explained in reductionist terms, then neither can the universe of which human persons are a part. The universe, like persons, is more than mechanism. Although a vast array of data can be assembled about the universe, we cannot ultimately understand the universe *as* lists of data. J.R. Illingworth, in a book published nearly a century ago, was already making this point. Commenting on the view that *prima facie* nature would incline us to materialism, he contends that the reverse is true: *prima facie* experience of nature leads to holistic spiritual experience, and it is only when we dig behind this holistic experience to discover its component parts that we can develop a materialistic theory.

But in doing so we pass from a whole to a partial view. The *prima facie* view is the judgement of our personality as a whole, in contact with nature as a whole; that is, a judgement in which our entire being takes part. But the analytic or scientific view is a partial view, with important elements left out; it makes abstraction, for its own purpose, of certain properties of things and omits the remainder.[18]

Such abstraction is proper and necessary for many purposes, but it should not be regarded as the whole story.

But how do we *know* that it is not the whole story? In this context, I have merely rejected reductionism as an account of personhood and of the universe, without giving a justification for doing so. Yet in an age after Feuerbach, Freud and Marx, some such justification is needed. While that is important, however, it can be set on one side for the present discussion, since the concern for this book has been to work out a theologically adequate account of the relationship between God and the universe from within a broadly Christian theological framework. In *that* framework, reductionism cannot find a place; it is not a position compatible with Christian theology. If, therefore, we begin from the shared theistic premise (which in another context cries out for justification) that reductionism cannot

18. J. R. Illingworth *Divine Immanence: An Essay on the Spiritual Significance of Matter* pp. 62–3.

be an adequate account of human persons, embodied though they are, then we have a concept of human immanence and transcendence which can provide a helpful model by which to understand the relationship between God and the universe.

For, if we affirm the transcendence of God, what we are affirming is that God is not reducible to the physical universe: ultimate reality is not describable in solely mechanistic terms. But, just as human persons are embodied but yet transcendent, so also the universe can be the body of a transcendent God. If human embodiment does not reduce personal significance to physiology, neither would the postulate that God's body is the universe mean that God is finally describable in exclusively physical terms. If this is correct, then transcendence is compatible with divine embodiment.

If transcendence is thus understood as the opposite of reductionism, rather than as the opposite of immanence, then a genuine and theologically fruitful conjunction of transcendence and immanence can be proposed. The enormous religious significance of both can be maintained without resorting to an embarrassed shuffle between two apparently contradictory poles. If the universe is thought of as God's body then the doctrine of divine immanence takes on obvious significance with enormous impact on our views of nature, science and technology, the human body, and the fine arts – to mention only a few areas too easily relegated to the 'secular'. And as long as we maintain that God cannot be reduced to the universe, the doctrine of transcendence is also important in our concept of the divine nature. I am not suggesting that this account of immanence and transcendence exhausts their philosophical or religious significance: quite the contrary, it opens up new paths for exploration. But it does provide a perspective from which such exploration can begin, instead of leaving immanence and transcendence at hopeless variance with one another.

It is important to be clear that this is not a reversion to metaphysical dualism. It is a repudiation of the suggestion that if God is not reducible to the universe, though the universe is God's body, this means that God is composed of two parts, his body and his incorporeal soul. If that were what was meant, we would have lapsed right back into all the problems of dualism and incorporeality that the idea of divine embodiment was intended to circumvent. But if we keep the human model firmly before us we shall be less likely to revert to dualism: to say that a human being is not reducible to his or her bodily functions and the impulses from the environment is, after all, not an expression of dualism but an alternative to it.

127

Whatever exactly is included in human transcendence, it is not a doctrine which posits, in Cartesian fashion, a thinking and unextended soul mysteriously interacting with an extended mechanical body. Instead, the notion of transcendence takes personhood as primary, and understands by personhood the framework within which the physical and the non-physical aspects of being human can be placed.

But numerous theologians have missed this point. There has been a considerable swing away from the monarchical ideas of deity which cosmic dualism brings in its train, a recognition that this picture of a God standing over against the world is a deistic model not suitable for Christian theology. Furthermore, there is nothing new about basing a revised understanding of the relationship between God and the universe on a doctrine of man, and using the human model to show how immanence and transcendence can be fruitfully conjoined. I have already referred to J.R. Illingworth and his emphasis on holistic explanation. He also emphasized the importance of seeing human persons as wholes: the basis for his entire account of divine immanence and transcendence is that, whatever our philosophy about spirit and matter, we never in fact experience them other than in combination. He says;

> On this analogy, then, the divine presence which we recognize in nature will be the presence of a Spirit, which infinitely transcends the material order, yet sustains and indwells it the while.[19]

But Illingworth soon lapses into an equivocation. He starts, as we did, by contrasting transcendence with reductionism, not with immanence, using the model of a human person. But he slides from this definition of transcendence as not *reducible* to mechanistic materialism to a definition of transcendence as something *other* than matter – literally (one is tempted to say spatially) over and above matter. But this is an unnecessary slide right back into the cosmic dualism which his book was intended to counteract, and is out of step with the human model of transcendence, which specifically does not posit an incorporeal extra something of another substance than the body.

John Macquarrie has been one of the leading voices in contemporary theology who called for an understanding of God and the world on a more organic, holistic model, rather than after the image of Pharaoh. Yet Macquarrie also, like Illingworth, slips from

19. Ibid., p. 72.

transcendence as 'not reducible' to something that sounds very much like transcendence as 'another substance'. There is still, in his view, an asymmetry between God and the world, and this asymmetry is expressed not simply in terms of the asymmetry between a person and his or her body where we would say that the concept of personhood includes *more* than the concept of physicality, but in the language of otherness: as though a person were *other* than his or her body in an ontological sense which cannot escape dualism. He says:

> In calling God 'transcendent' we mean that he is other than the world, indeed that there belongs to him a different order of being ... The concept of transcendence implies therefore that there is an element of asymmetry in God's relation to the world.[20]

However, the asymmetry which Macquarrie rightly wishes to preserve can be preserved without reverting to the notion that God is somehow 'over and above' the world, other than the world in the way that a Cartesian soul is other than and over and above a physical body. If one can reject both Cartesianism and reductionism in favour of a holistic concept which includes the transcendence of human persons, one can similarly escape cosmic dualism without falling into materialistic mechanism in giving an account of the transcendence of God.

A particularly striking example of a theologian struggling with a holistic concept of the relationship between God and the physical world is A.R. Peacocke. Aware of the dangers inherent in a sharply drawn contrast between them, Peacocke proposed a biological model, which has the additional merit of taking seriously the need to see God in female terms as well as male:

> The concept of God as Creator has, in the past, been too much dominated by a stress on the externality of God's creative acts – he is regarded as creating something external to himself, just as the male fertilizes the womb from the outside. But mammalian females, at least, create within themselves and the growing embryo resides within the female body and this is a proper corrective to the masculine picture – it is an analogy of God creating the world within herself, we would have to say.[21]

The idea of God as Mother, holding the emergent world in her

20. John Macquarrie *Principles of Christian Theology* p. 120.
21. Arthur Peacocke *Creation and the World of Science* p. 142.

womb, is indeed a very much needed corrective to the sexually biased portrayal of God as dominant male. But this does not get us very much further for Peacocke's purpose of coming to a clearer understanding of transcendence and immanence. Indeed, it very vividly portrays transcendence as something 'over and above': the relationship of a mother to an embryo developing in her womb is a very different relationship, at least in its later stages, from that of a woman to her own body. Although the foetus is in some sense flesh of her flesh, her otherness, her distinctness from it, grows more and more pronounced until the day when there are literally two distinct entities. If this is the model for divine transcendence, then only reluctance to bring the model to birth can save us from cosmic dualism.

Nevertheless, one of the reasons why Macquarrie, Peacocke and others emphasize ontological otherness, a dualistic idea of transcendence, is that part of the meaning of transcendence is that God could exist without the world; he is logically (and perhaps temporally) prior to the world, because he is its Creator. As such, it might be thought that he could not be related to the world as a person is to his body, since no matter how strongly we insist that a person transcends physicality, he or she cannot be said to create a body or even to antedate it. Thus it is important to turn to an account of the doctrine of creation, to see how it, too, is illuminated by the model of God embodied.

130

7

Creation: The One and the Many

1. Creation

Whatever the doctrine of creation is, it is not a scientific explanation for the origin of universes. The function of a scientific explanation of any event is to give an account of how that event can be subsumed under a general law, or of how it can be inferred by piecing together other general laws. Clearly, however, we do not have available any general laws about the origin of universes, and if we did, they would not be theological doctrines. The doctrine of creation *ex nihilo* is, at this level, rather a theistic label to the mystery of why there should be something rather than nothing; a label which, though it solves no scientific problems, points to God (rather than to, say, blind chance) as the terminating point of our inquiry. This is not meant as a repudiation of natural theology, but rather as a recognition of the difference between giving scientific explanation, which is typically couched in terms of laws, mechanisms, and so on, and a personal or theistic one, which is not.

No matter how strong a form is given to the doctrine of creation, it can at best account for the origin of the existence of everything *except* God: creation *ex nihilo* posits God as the ultimate origin of all things, but it cannot by definition say anything about his origin too. This is why the question 'Who made God?' counts as a decisive refutation of the cosmological argument, if that argument is taken in the sense of giving a proof of the existence of God from the felt need to explain why anything exists. Any creationist account of the origin of the universe is bound to leave unexplained the origin of the Creator himself – no one seriously thinks God's existence can be explained by saying that God created himself, though saying that God is self-caused comes perilously near such an attempt and is for that reason an undesirable way of putting things.

However, the idea that God created the universe at a temporal point, before which he existed without it, has been a perplexing notion for centuries, even for those who wish to retain a radical ontological distinction between God and the world. As we saw in our discussion about God and time, there were debates about what God might have been doing before he created the world. Nor were such debates frivolous, for what they were really seeking was some reason why God should have engaged in creative activity at all if he had previously not done so. If no reason can be given, it would seem that creation was an arbitary whim; on the other hand if there is a reason, then why was that reason not eternally valid – why did God create the world when he did and not sooner? Now, if God is not timeless but everlasting, then the questions concerning the temporal beginning of the universe arise in an even more acute manner, and it seems that any answer involves us in a doctrine of divine capriciousness. Thus it is necessary to reconsider the premise that God created the world at some point in time, to see whether it might be possible to understand a creative relationship of God to the world in some way other than creation *ex nihilo* 'in the beginning'. I shall suggest one such way, which is made possible by the postulate that the world is the embodiment of God, and which allows us to retain what is theologically important in the doctrine of creation. There are two related aspects to this suggestion, which will be clearer if they are treated separately.

(1) The Universe (or its basic ingredients) has always existed; creation does not mean bringing the basic stuff into existence but rather forming it, making it a cosmos rather than a chaos.

(2) The Universe is absolutely dependent upon God for its existence (if God did not exist, neither could the universe) but this is an eternal dependence, not one which had a temporal beginning.

(1) A major impetus to the view that creation should be understood as God's formative work on pre-existent matter comes from Plato's *Timaeus*, whose enormous influence on early and medieval theology has become apparent in earlier chapters. In the *Timaeus*, the world as we know it is explained as the work of the Demiurge, who works like a craftsman on pre-existent and somewhat recalcitrant matter, making it as good as he can. From the point of view of accurate scholarship, it is a highly dubious move to baptize the god of the *Timaeus* and convert him by force into the God of Christian theology. But dubious or not, such christening took place in the early history of Christian thought. It may have been begun or at least facilitated by Justin Martyr, who believed that the Greek philosophers, especially Plato, had many true doctrines, but that they had derived these from the Hebrew scriptures which they had only partially understood. Particularly with reference to creation, Justin at one point explicitly accepts that creation is the work of God on pre-existent matter; he says 'and we have been taught that he in the beginning did of his goodness, for man's sake, create all things out of unformed matter',[1] and Justin thinks that this point was taken over from the Old Testament by the Greeks.

It was possible for thinkers of his time to take such a point of view on the doctrine of creation because, although in our time the idea that creation was *ex nihilo* is firmly embedded in the tradition of the Church thanks to Fathers like Augustine, it is nowhere directly stated in the Bible. Since this is so, the early Fathers presumably felt free to take whatever line they found most convincing. And given the prevailing Platonic view of matter which saw it as at least partially responsible for evil, the idea that God worked with recalcitrant matter would help explain evil without attributing it to God, and would also provide a basis for practical morality. The pagan philosopher Plotinus, writing at the close of the third century, explicitly said that pre-existing matter was the source of evil in the world, and in consequence advocated a life-style of persevering asceticism as an effort to free the soul from the shackles of the material body.[2] This, taken over into Christian thought, became part of the motivation for Christian asceticism and monasticism long after such ideas of creation had been officially repudiated. That is another story, but it takes its beginning in the negative view of matter and a radically dualistic attitude towards the relationship between God and the world, and helps to illustrate the extent to which the ancient theories of the nature of matter entered into Christian thought and practice.

If creation is seen as God's action on pre-existent matter, and we use metaphors like craftsman, potter and clay, or the like, then creation is quite compatible with the idea of an embodied Creator – indeed the metaphors suggest it – though that Creator would be distinct from the material upon which he worked. However, the Fathers encountered great difficulties with this view of creation as divine craftsmanship, and the Church eventually rejected it in favour of the doctrine of creation *ex nihilo*. Irenaeus, speaking against the Gnostics, said:

> They do not believe that God (being powerful, and rich in all resources) created matter itself, inasmuch as they do not know how much a spiritual and divine essence can accomplish . . .

1. Justin Martyr *Apology* X; cf. *Hortatory Address to the Greeks* XX, XXIX – XXXIII.
2. Plotinus *Enneads* I.4; I. 8. 5.

While men, indeed, cannot make anything out of nothing, but only out of matter already existing, yet God is in this point pre-eminently superior to men, that he himself called into being the substance of his creation, when previously it had no existence.[3]

And there is an issue of great importance underlying this statement. If God had created only in the sense of forming and shaping pre-existent matter, God would not be sovereign. There would be something external to him which limited him – he could in a sense do nothing about it, at least, not about its existence and basic nature. Even his omnipotence and creative ability would be restricted to the material with which he must work. And although such limitation might be turned to theological purpose to explain the existence of evil, the price to be paid is much too high. For if evil is grounded in independently existing matter, outside the will or control of God, then although this would give an intellectual explanation of it, it would also make its abolition for ever impossible so long as anything material remained. It would be preferable to leave the problem of evil perpetually unsolved than to attribute it to pre-existent matter and thus, while solving the intellectual difficulties about its existence, end with no hope of ever getting rid of it.

The idea of God as a craftsman working on pre-existent matter also posits, with the independence of matter, a cosmic dualism of such striking contrast between God and the world that it was considered heretical, not Christian. Even though theologians have insisted on an essential distinction between God and the world, traditionally this otherness has not been conceived of as total independence, but as a created difference: ultimately all things come from God.

Now, if we think of the universe as the embodiment of God, we can take these two themes of the sovereignty of God and the independence of all things upon him, and combine them with the ancient idea of God as craftsman, to develop a theologically rich doctrine of creation which does not founder on the problem of evil. For if the universe is God's body, then all of it, everything that exists, is God's self-expression. It is God's self-formation, and owes its being what it is directly to God's formative will. As we have already seen, there is a disanalogy between God's relationship to the universe and our relationship to our bodies, in that our bodies are not in every respect the function of our wills. They are to a certain extent expressive of us, but in many other respects they are

3. Irenaeus *Against Heresies* II.X. 3–4; cf. XIV.4.

given: we cannot by taking thought make one hair white or black. But God is in complete control of the universe; nothing exists apart from his will. Far from showing that God is a disembodied spirit, this points rather to what I have called more complete embodiment. We are embodied only incompletely, in the sense that our bodies are only partially expressive of ourselves, our desires and attitudes. But God expresses himself completely in the universe, in the sense that there is nothing in the universe which for him is a mere given, over which he has no control; each aspect of the physical universe is as he wills it to be. Thus everything that exists is created by God and absolutely dependent upon him in just the same sense if the universe is God's body as it is if the doctrine of creation *ex nihilo* is true, except that God formed it quite literally 'out of himself' – that is, it is his self-formation – rather than out of nothing. The doctrine of creation *ex nihilo* was, as we saw, adopted partly to preserve the doctrine of God's sovereignty: it was considered incorrect to think that things could exist without God having made them and hence not in dependence upon God. But if all that exists is in a quite literal sense the self-manifestation of God, then it is clearly not in any way independent of him, as it would be on a Platonic-type theory of pre-existent matter. It would be, literally, God's creative self-manifestation.

But would this not mean that the universe and everything in it would have to be eternal? Nothing could be created or destroyed without adding or subtracting to the totality of God. This objection, however, is misguided. It is true that, if the universe is the embodiment of God, then the universe taken as a whole must be everlasting; we will shortly return to this point. But that is a very different thing from saying that the universe as we now perceive it, or the individual things within it, must be everlasting. God could utterly eradicate its current formation and actualize something unimaginably different if he so chose:

This does not exclude the possibility that there is another side from us to the 'hot big bang'. Beyond this point, when the 'universe is squeezed through a knot hole', all physical constants might have been different – even though all such extrapolation is speculative and hazardous. So that the nuclear- and electronic-energy levels of the atoms of carbon, nitrogen, hydrogen, oxygen, and phosphorus on which living matter, as we know it, is so utterly dependent, would be different. Indeed these atoms, or even atoms as such, might not be constituent units of the universe on the 'other side' of the condensed gravitational mass from which our present observable universe expanded. So we have to envisage the possibility that our universe (the one which has allowed the emergence of life, and so of man) is but one amongst a, possibly infinite, cycle of universes.[4]

Obviously this is speculative, but it is speculation consistent with both science and a theology which takes God's freedom and sovereignty seriously. If the universe is God's body, God's self-formation, and he is in complete control of it, then he can change it in whatever way he chooses. The existence of each thing is utterly dependent upon God for both its origin and its continued existence.

The idea of creation *ex nihilo* could not in any case be taken to mean that in the beginning there was something, namely nothing, from which God created the world! The point of the doctrine is rather that the origin of all things is in God, not in some principle extraneous to God. And this is preserved in the idea that God created the universe and its contents out of himself, as his self-formation since it could then hardly be thought of as a being or principle other than or in opposition to God. Further, the doctrine of creation *ex nihilo* was meant to guard against a danger inherent in emanationist theories that God is reduced or diminished by his creation of the world. But this, again, is unproblematic if the creation is not something other than God, but a self-formation of God's body, since if this is so, God is clearly not diminished by it.

This brings us back to a problem raised in an earlier chapter. If the point of the doctrine of creation *ex nihilo* is not that things are partly indebted to nothingness for their existence, but rather that everything owes its origin and continuation to God, then the problem of evil takes an acute form. For it means, as we saw earlier, that evil must not be simply a force opposed to God and external to him, but must actually find its origin in God himself.

We noted earlier that the position that both good and evil are present in God is not unknown in Christian thought: Jakob Boehme wrestled with the implications of this. But in any case, anyone who retained the traditional model of creation and said that the world and everything in it is created *ex nihilo,* and that there is no other external principle besides God, would also make God in some sense responsible for evil. One need not, and indeed should not, think of evil as a *thing* which God could have created or not, in the way that he could have created the moon or not as he chose. But even though

4. A.R. Peacocke *Creation and the World of Science* p. 69.

evil ought not to be reified in that way, it is still true that unless there is some eternal principle other than God, God is ultimately responsible for evil. This is true whether creation is thought to be literally out of *nothing* or, in the sense I have suggested, out of *God*.

It would be morally and intellectually reprehensible to pretend that evil is not really a problem for theism. What I am suggesting, however, is that in the context of trying to understand the doctrine of creation the same conclusion holds as we came to in discussing divine agency: the problem of evil is not *more* of a problem to one who believes that the universe is God's body than it is to one who believes that an immaterial God created everything out of nothing and sustains it by his will. In either case, God wills or permits evil, and in either case a theodicy is necessary. The advance of either over the Platonic thought of a Demiurge working on pre-existent matter, or a Babylonian cosmogonic myth which includes the birth of the gods themselves, is that since evil is not in some principle anterior to or independent of God there is some hope that it may be overcome. For the evil does not lie in matter itself, so that it could never be eradicated as long as matter exists. Whatever theodicy we come to, this is now excluded in favour of a view that God permits evil for a time, for some specific purpose, after which it will be overcome. If evil is to be seen as a consequence of the free will of persons (and this usually forms at least part of efforts to explain it) this will hold in just the same way if the universe is the embodiment of God as it would if it had been created *ex nihilo*. If the creation is God's self-manifestation, furthermore, then the evil which is now a part of it is shared by him rather than inflicted from on high.

(2) Another way of reconsidering the doctrine of creation *ex nihilo* is to return to the question, 'When did God make it?' If we think of the universe as the embodiment of God, then our answer to this question will be that the world and everything in it is absolutely dependent upon God for its existence – and always has been. If God did not exist, neither would the universe. But the world did not have a beginning in time; it has always existed, and its various forms are various expressions of God. God is not merely an external originating impulse for the existence of the world – that would in any case be Deism, not Christianity, which understands creation as a continuous relation of ontological dependence between Creator and creation.

There would be an obvious theological advantage to this view of creation based upon the model of the world as God's body. For if one said that creation happened, instead, at some moment in the

137

distant past, one is presumably committed to the belief that God existed incorporeally and everlastingly *before* that time. Then, as we have seen, the question haunts us: why did God, having gone on for everlasting ages without a world, finally create one? What prompted him to do it? It is hard not to slip into a mental picture of God finally becoming bored or lonely with his endless existence and so deciding to create a world as a diversion from the tedium of eternity. One can of course paint this picture in much brighter theological colours, describing God's essentially loving and relational character which expresses itself, though not out of need. Yet that leaves the question of why he did it then and not sooner unresolved, and produces either evasion or sheer admission that we cannot have any hint of the inscrutable actions and motivations of God.

It might be possible to develop a response to this, however, along the following lines. The nearest analogy we have to divine creativity is human creativity: painting, writing a poem, inventing something. Now, these creative events are temporal, and are the self-expression of their human creators, but it is misguided to ask for an explanation of why they took place just when they did, not earlier or later. 'What a beautiful painting; why didn't you paint it sooner?' would be a very peculiar comment to make to an artist when his masterpiece was unveiled. But if we cannot properly raise such a question about human creativity, why should we think it appropriate to raise it about divine creation?

However, there is more to be said here. It is not the case that we can never properly ask temporal questions about human creativity: good biographies of painters and poets and inventors tell us a good deal about the antecedents to their creative work, and the changes in the characters of the artists without which their art would be inconceivable. It makes good sense to say that Picasso could not have painted 'Guernica' had it not been for his experiences of the Spanish Civil War and its effects on his character, or Henry James written *Portrait of a Lady* before he himself experienced disillusionment and loss of innocence. These events deeply shaped the subsequent self-expression of the artists; so deeply that one might almost say that after these events there was a different 'self' to express because of their impact. In general, profound creativity at a human level usually has profound experience or insight as its antecedent. So if the question, 'Why didn't you paint it sooner?' is misguided, this does not mean that the question, 'What caused you to paint it when you did?' let alone the question 'Why did you choose to paint at all?' is equally misguided. If there were no formative influences whatever which led up to new forms of self-expression in a particular case, we should be very puzzled. Similarly, if God at some point in time created the universe, never before having expressed himself in any similar way, it makes sense to ask why he did so.

The problem is that any answer sufficient to explain why God created at all – answers such as God's goodness, God's overflowing love, and the like – will then be pressed to explain why these reasons, if sufficient, were not sufficient eternally. It would seem that one would either have to attribute creation to an arbitrary decision on God's part, or else say that there was some change in God's nature, some extensive thought process which finally culminated in a decision to create, or some cause outside of God which prompted him to act. But none of these alternatives seem theologically satisfying.

It was partly as a solution to these very problems that Augustine and others proposed the doctrine that God is timeless. As we saw when we discussed the idea of timelessness, the very notion of time involves the created phenomenal world: before the creation of the world, there could be no such thing as time. So it is a misunderstanding of the nature of time which leads to a puzzle about what God was doing before he created the world. When once this misunderstanding is cleared away, the foolishness of the question is apparent and the problem evaporates.

But this solution, ingenious as it is, is not satisfactory. We have already seen that it does not make sense to speak of God as timeless. But even waiving that point, Augustine's answer would not solve anything. Suppose we granted for the sake of argument that God is timeless and that he created time when he created the world (or, more accurately, that time began with God's creation of the world). This still leaves us with the question of why God created it at all. If any sufficient reason for creation can be given, why was that reason not eternally sufficient? It is difficult to phrase the question without begging the question of timelessness. Yet even Augustine would want to say that the universe did not always exist: but if it did not always exist, why did it ever begin to exist, and what did God do when he existed but the universe did not? The same old questions keep recurring. Perhaps the best answer to the question of what God did when he existed but the world did not is still the one attributed to Luther's variation on a theme from Augustine: he sat under a willow tree and cut switches for people who would ask impertinent questions.

A latter-day Augustine might be able to provide a better answer, but I do not know how to put it into his mouth. It seems a more promising approach to suggest that the world in fact always existed, though of course in many forms previous to the one we now know, in dependence on the goodness and sovereignty of God who continuously wills its being. A tentative step in this direction was taken by Thomas Aquinas. Aquinas himself clearly believed that the world did not always exist; but he held this as an article of faith and expressly denied that it could be demonstrated. Referring to some ancient philosophers spoken of by Augustine, he says:

> . . . they hold that the world has a beginning, not of time, but of creation, which means that . . . it was ever made. They try to explain themselves as follows. Were a foot, they say, in the dust from eternity there would always be a footprint there and nobody could doubt that it had been imprinted by him who trod there, so likewise the world always was because he who made it always existed.[5]

Although Aquinas had already made clear that he believed that the world has not always existed because this has been divinely revealed, he does not dismiss the view of eternal creation as nonsense. Rather, he tries to elucidate it as follows:

> For the explanation: we agree that an efficient cause which works through change must precede its effects in time, for the effect enters as the term of the action whereas the agent is its start. Yet in the event of the action being instantaneous and not successive, it is not required for the maker to be prior to the thing made, as appears in the case of illumination. Hence they point out that because God is the active cause of the world, it does not follow that he is prior to it in duration, for . . . creation, whereby he produced the world, is not successive change.[6]

Thomas Aquinas did not have in mind the sort of everlasting ontological dependence of the world upon God which I have been suggesting; but he did realize that it is only on the basis of revelation that we could say that the world had a temporal beginning, even when it has already been granted that God is its creator. And since our understanding of the nature and content of the early chapters of Genesis is different from that of Aquinas, we have all the more

5. Thomas Aquinas *Summa Theologiae* Ia. 46. 2 Reply to Obj. 1.
6. Ibid.

reason for taking seriously the idea that creation is a relationship of eternal dependence.

Christian theologians, indeed, have a precedent for this view in the doctrine of the eternal generation of the Son, which must be understood on roughly similar lines. The Son has always been ontologically dependent upon the Father; yet there was never a time when the Father was not the Father – that is, at no time did he not generate the Son. It may be that this doctrine is more Greek than biblical (and it finds striking parallel in the notion of Plotinus of the eternal emanation of the Nous from the One); but it has become a respected strand of Trinitarian theology. And if God is eternally Father in virtue of eternally generating the Son – so that there is a relationship of ontological dependence but not temporal sequence – then we could similarly say that God is the eternal Creator of the world, though the world is ontologically dependent upon God. The further causal relationship between God and the world can be interpreted as formative causality, in which God makes everything that exists as his self-expression. Nor does this mean that the world would have equal dignity with the Son: dignity is after all not a simple question of temporal priority and there is still all the difference between formation and generation, creating and begetting. The universe may be understood as God's *body*, but the Son must be understood as in some sense God's *person*.

If this account of God's relationship with the universe is taken seriously, then, although the universe could have passed through many different forms, it must always have existed in some form or other; *some* universe must always have existed, and must exist for ever in the future. To put this into the frame of reference provided by the human model, if embodiment is a necessary condition for personhood then if the body ceases to exist, so does the person. Of course, the body need not continue in its present *form:* it may be that there is a resurrection from the dead, for instance. But if God is to the universe as a person is to his or her body, then would we not have to say that God is dependent on the world just as much as the world is dependent on God? How could this be consistent with omnipotence?

This problem may be solved by closer attention to the concept of dependence. Normally when we say that x is dependent on y the implication is that x and y are two different entities; thus a man might depend on his friend for help or information or moral support. Now, if x cannot get along without y, if y's help or information is necessary to x, then the dependence takes a very strong form, and we might say that without y, x would be helpless, ignorant, or sad. But our dependence upon our bodies is quite different from this. It is not simply that we would be weakened or incapacitated without our bodies: without our bodies we would not *be*. Our bodies are not something other than ourselves upon which, as it happens, we depend for various purposes. Our bodies, rather, are an aspect of ourselves, and although it is mistaken to say that a person is nothing but his or her body, that is not to say that a person is something separate or separable from his or her body, but that body is to be understood within the wider concept of personhood. But if embodiment is a necessary aspect of what it is to be a person, then although in that sense it is right to say that our existence depends upon our bodies (since if our bodies did not exist or had never been conceived, neither would we) this is not the same sort of dependence as depending on someone else's strength rather than being self-sufficient.

Similarly if the universe is God's body then there must be a universe if there is a God; and if God is eternal, so is the universe (though again, not its present arrangement). To think of this as a dependence which undermines omnipotence or self-sufficiency, however, is to think of the universe as ontologically other than God, something external to God on which God must depend for his existence. But we can now see that such a line of thought begs the question. If the universe is God's 'self' in a sense analogous to the way my body is my self – that is, not something external to me or other than me – then God's dependence on the universe does not undercut his self-sufficiency: God depends on nothing but himself. The problem only arises if we assume, contrary to the hypothesis, that the universe is something other than God, not his body. If it is his body, then his dependence on it is self-dependence, and that, far from being a denial of omnipotence, is its necessary condition.

This point can be made another way. Suppose that we hold to the sort of ontological division which might be attributed to Descartes or Locke, holding that there are three sorts of substances: material substance, mental substance, and divine substance – bodies, minds, and God. Now if any of these depended on any other, then that other was ontologically prior; for Berkeley, for example, mental substance took priority over material bodies because he believed that *esse est percipi*. But for an entity to be dependent on its own substance would not be dependence in the same sense: it would be more accurate, for instance, to say that a mind is an instantiation of mental substance than that it is dependent on mental substance, for although there would be no minds if there were no mental

142

substance, the converse is true as well: minds just are individuals of mental substance for Berkeley. Again, no one supposes that there could be divine substance without God or God without divine substance; these are not two possible entities but one. So although there is a sense in which one might say that God's existence depends on the existence of divine substance, this really amounts to saying that God exists if he exists. If the universe is God's body, then although God would not exist if the universe did not, this does not threaten his omnipotence, for it only means that the universe is the physical aspect of God, that God and the universe are one reality, not two. In the beginning of the chapter I said that whatever we mean by creation *ex nihilo* we do not mean that God created himself. We can now see why this is important. If the universe is God's body, an aspect of the reality of God, then it is eternal, but this no more challenges God's omnipotence or sovereignty than the fact that God does not create himself – indeed, it is part of the same fact.

It is also important to keep in mind, in this connection, the disanalogy between God's embodiment and our own. As already discussed, our bodies are only partially subject to our voluntary control: it is a general 'given' that persons are embodied, but there are specific 'givens' as well, like our organic structure, the parameters of our height and weight, our sex, and so on. But I have suggested that God is more completely embodied than we are; that is, the specific aspects of the universe are not, for him, givens but are his voluntary self-expression. Thus the universe is dependent upon God in a sense in which he is not dependent upon it; each particular thing owes its creation and continued existence to his gracious will. This is the important truth in John Macquarrie's emphasis on the asymmetry between God and the world, but it does not imply any dualistic 'over and above' idea of God.

But could not God will, not just that this or that particular thing cease to exist but that the whole universe cease? Could not God 'slough off' the universe in a way in which we cannot 'slough off' our bodies? If the universe is God's body, then the response must be that he cannot abolish it unless he can also abolish himself: if God were to will the annihilation of the universe then he would be willing his own annihilation, analogous to the way in which destruction of our bodies is self-destruction. Of course God could utterly transform the universe, making 'a new heaven and a new earth', but that is not the question here. Rather, what is in question is whether God could commit suicide. Whether the universe is ultima-

143

tely destructible amounts to asking whether and in what sense God
is a necessary being. Pursuing this issue would take us too far afield.

As a matter of fact, there are strong theological reasons for saying
that God and the universe must be coeternal: traditional theology,
though it sometimes claims that God could slough off the universe,
also gives reason to question that claim. In the first place, all the
questions that arise if we say that the universe had a beginning in
time reappear if we postulate that it could have an end in time: any
reason sufficient for creation would seem to be sufficient not only
for all ages past, but álso for all ages future. It is worth noticing in
this connection that the first attribute of God which the Bible points
to, and one which is fundamental to the Judaeo-Christian concept
of God, is that God is Creator. But creativity, if it is an essential
attribute and not an external insignificant activity, does not express
itself only in one isolated act. If God is eternally a creative God,
then his creativity would express itself eternally. The same thing
can be said about God as Revealer, Self-communicator. If God is
the one who manifests himself, if that is not just a temporary
accidental property but rather an expression of what God is really
like, then it makes no sense to postulate either a temporal beginning
or a temporal end-point to this self-manifestation: he who is eternally the Revealer must reveal himself eternally.

But the most telling point is that God as portrayed in the Gospel
accounts of Jesus' conception of him is above everything else a God
of love. For the writers of the New Testament, this is the most
significant thing that can be said about God, and it is within
the context of God's love that all other divine attributes must be
understood and modified. But love that loves nothing is impossible.
If God is essentially and eternally love, then God must have loved
eternally. He has not existed for endless ages in isolation, nor can
he look forward to a long solitary retirement after the duties of this
workaday world are done and the universe disposed of. Rather,
he has poured himself out, and will continue to do so, in loving
manifestations of himself, in ways which, doubtless, we cannot even
guess.

But if this is correct, if God has always loved and always will, if
there must always be a universe, a self-manifestation of love, then,
on the one hand, God's relationship to the universe is very intimate
indeed, and yet on the other there must be finite responsive individuals who are not God to love. This raises a paradox. If the universe
is God's eternal self-expression, God's body, this seems to imply
pantheism. Yet if there are finite recipients of God's love, able to

love in response, they must have individuality and autonomy. This is the paradox that will occupy us in the remaining two sections of this chapter.

2. The One

An inward spirit feeds earth, heaven and sea,
The shining moon, and giant stars; a mind
Pervades their limbs, and moves the mighty mass.[7]

Poets have been speaking in this way for centuries. And for centuries, such poetic licence has been taken as an expression of religious devotion, as a communion through the sacrament of nature with nature's God. But only if it is not taken literally. If the poet is using words like these to express God's creativity and sovereignty and wisdom, they are acceptable; but should he insist that they are meant quite soberly, that earth, sea, and moon really are the limbs of God, then he has lapsed into pantheism.

We have already encountered instances where indiscriminate use of a blanket term smothers a live issue, and 'pantheist' is another such term. It has, in Karl Rahner's phrase, become a 'heresy label', as though its application were sufficient to settle theological questions. But when we examine its contents more closely, we find that there is a good deal to be learned from it (as we should have expected from an idea that has refused to die) and that that part of it which must in the end be rejected as incompatible with divine transcendence is not the idea that the world is the embodiment of God.

There is a curious sense in which the distrust evoked in modern times by the idea of pantheism is akin to that which worried the early Fathers of Christendom. The Stoics, whom the Fathers took to be the primary advocates of pantheism, were as profoundly impressed as are post-Enlightenment scientists with natural law and the order in the natural world. This led them to formulate deterministic and mechanistic world-views, similar to those of early modern determinists like Spinoza. But if such a mechanistic, deterministic universe is God, as such an interpretation of pantheism would be bound to affirm, then God would be reduced to the physical system. There would be no possibility of ascribing agency or a personal nature to God. God would simply be the system itself, transcribable without remainder into quantitative formulae if we

7. Virgil *Aeneid* VI. 724.

only had the requisite mathematical sophistication. In fact, this is a caricature of the thought of the Stoics (and of Spinoza) but in this context that is unimportant. The point is that this was what the popularized idea of pantheism conveyed: the natural order was then seen as a picture best described by mechanics, determinism, and impersonal objectivity. And it is little wonder that anyone who maintains that the first thing we must say about God is that he is love, as Christians do, must recoil from the suggestion that God is to be identified with such a universe. This would amount to giving up everything significant in our idea of God.

It is this line of thinking that Locke pursues in his attempt to refute the idea that God could be material. After giving a version of the cosmological argument for the existence of God, he proceeds to show that the Creator of the cosmos, eternal wisdom, must be incorporeal spirit. He first considers whether rationality could arise out of matter:

> . . . Let us suppose the matter of the next pebble we meet with, eternal, closely united, and the parts firmly at rest together, if there were no other being in the world, must it not eternally remain so, a dead, inactive lump?[8]

Matter itself can only be thought of as extended and hence divisible stuff: irrespective of how small the particles into which it is divided, they still do nothing but 'knock, impell, and resist one another'. It would be ludicrous to think that this was God.

Nevertheless, we are thinking beings and we have material bodies: could the material universe be the body of God? As Locke phrases it, would it not be possible that the 'eternal thinking being is material'? He argues that this is equally preposterous. In the first place, he asserts that one could not possibly hold that every single minute particle of matter thinks, for this would mean that 'there would be as many eternal thinking beings, as there are particles of matter, and so an infinity of gods'. But if it is absurd to suppose that all particles of matter think, then no reason could be given, either why one particle should think unlike all the other particles from which it does not otherwise differ, or, more pertinently, why an aggregate of particles should do so:

> For unthinking particles of matter, however put together, can have nothing thereby added to them, but a new relation of posi-

8. John Locke *An Essay Concerning Human Understanding* IV. X. 10.

tion, which 'tis impossible should give thought and knowledge to them.[9]

But this argument is invalid, and Locke should have seen it. It is false that a thing can be no more than the sum of its parts. Locke must have had as a model something like grains of sand on a seashore: no matter how many grains you add, it is still only a heap of sand, never a palm tree, and the grains only 'knock, impell, and resist one another'. Yet palm trees do grow, and if Locke had chosen one of them, or something else organic, as his model, he would have been less easily misled into thinking that putting particles of matter together in a new way could not, with the new organization, engender new abilities as well: Locke, after all, did not think that palm trees had souls. It is indicative of the grip of the Cartesian idea of matter as utterly inert and without life or thought, that Locke, though he was a trained physician, should have thought of matter not as organic but as a 'dead, inactive lump'. Locke was capable of giving a cosmological argument and stressing the conceptual necessity of a creator God, and at the same time of thinking that matter is utterly alien to the nature of God, only because he had fixed ideas about the nature of matter and its antithesis to mind. One can only speculate about what Locke might have written had he lived at a time when Darwin, not Newton, could have been his scientific mentor.

Locke's real worries, which are at the root of his denial that God could be material, soon emerge:

> We cannot conceive how anything but impulse of body can move body; and yet that is not a reason sufficient to make us deny it possible, against the constant experience, we have of it in our selves, in all our voluntary motions, which are produced in us only by the free action or thought of our own minds; and are not, nor can be the effects of the impulse of determination of the motion of blind matter, in or upon our bodies; for then it could not be in our power to alter it.[10]

If the motion of matter, but for the overruling of an incorporeal mind, is nothing but the blind concatenation of forces, mechanistic and without the possibility of choice, then God could not be material on pain of surrendering to reductionism and determinism. Pantheism must be rejected, and the causal ability of mind

9. Ibid. IV. X. 16.
10. Ibid. IV. X. 19.

preserved, even though Locke is forced to admit that we cannot form a conception of the interaction of mind and body.

But now we can see that the real objection is not to pantheism itself, so much as to the reductionist materialism and determinism which it is thought to entail. But such an entailment would hold only if the material universe really is a 'dead, inactive lump', the impersonal mechanical structure which Descartes and his followers imagined it to be. But if, on the other hand, the universe is in some sense a meaningful whole, and an expression of divine will, love and creativity, such a reductionist programme cannot even get started.

Now, we cannot repudiate the data of science on behalf of theological speculation. But equally, this rigidly mechanical model of the universe is, as we have seen, far less acceptable to scientists themselves than theologians sometimes take for granted, especially as the life-sciences are growing in prominence and scientific thought is not dominated by the more explicitly quantitative sciences. If theologians retain ideas of the universe which regard it as mechanistic, deterministic and alien, something to be controlled rather than something to be understood and communed with, then the vigorous repudiation of pantheism is justified. Yet scientists themselves have been offering us food for thought about the extent to which such a model is adequate.

But for theologians the really decisive consideration against looking upon the world as an alien mechanism must come, surely, from theology itself. It is after all hardly a live option for a theology which holds to the doctrine that the world was created by a God who loves it and pronounces it good, to think of the world, God's self-expression, as an alien mechanism. Furthermore, we human beings, embodied as we are, are part of this universe – we therefore think of it as alien only at the cost of cutting an unbridgeable chasm not just between us and the rest of the universe, but within our very selves. The doctrine of creation can scarcely be maintained in any form without also maintaining that the world, ourselves included, is God's deliberate and loving self-expression. The universe cannot be utterly alien, impersonal and meaningless, but the personal and significant self-expression of God. Thinking in this way about the universe already removes much of the sting of pantheism.

When we consider pantheism in the light of creationist teaching, furthermore, we can see that it is reaching towards an important insight which is too easily ignored. As Paul Tillich puts it:

Pantheism is the doctrine that God is the substance or essence of all things, not the meaningless assertion that God is the totality of all things. The pantheistic element in the classical doctrine that God is *ipsum esse,* being-itself, is . . . necessary for a Christian doctrine of God.[11]

A theist who takes the doctrine of creation seriously must finally affirm, with the pantheist and against the reductionist, that all reality is from God and is ultimately not separable from him. There are not two sorts of reality, one of which is God and the other ontologically opposite to God; such was the teaching of the Manichees, and it was rejected by Christian theologians. This awareness that all things derive from God, that in the last analysis there can be nothing that exists outside of or other than God, is one of the elements in the often-repeated assertion that God is not a being among beings, an individual among other individuals. God is Being Itself, it is said, the source and ground of the existence of all things. In this sense every Christian theist is bound to be a monist, and it was this aspect of Spinozistic monism which was so attractive to the writers of the Romantic movement who reacted against the Enlightenment ideas of a mechanistic universe and the Deistic compromise which coupled such ideas with a doctrine of a remote, monarchical God. Thus Lessing, for instance, wrote: 'However I may seek to explain the reality of things outside God, I must confess that I can form no idea of it,'[12] and argued that things exist as ideas in God's mind, without which they would be nothing. This was also a major impetus towards Hegelian Absolute Idealism: the recognition that if there is a God at all, an omnipotent being to whom all else owes its existence, then God is All, there can in the absolute sense be nothing else. There is ample philosophical warrant for preferring the alternate reading which the translators of the New English Bible give for Ephesians 1:23: God 'appointed Christ. . . . to be all that he himself is who fills the universe in all its parts.'

If pantheism is thus understood as an affirmation that all reality is God's reality, that there can be nothing without God or utterly apart from him or independent of him, then pantheism is not an alternative to Christian theology but an ingredient in it. The idea of the universe as God's body draws out this aspect of pantheistic thought, stressing as it does God's immanence and totality while still

11. Paul Tillich *Systematic Theology* Vol. 1, p. 324.
12. G. E. Lessing 'On the Reality of Things Outside God' in Chadwick, pp. 102–3.

rejecting reductionist accounts which plunge us into mechanistic determinism.

Having said this, however, it is important to notice as well that the distrust of pantheism is not without some grounds: its regular and vehement repudiation, though often for inadequate reasons, should put us on our guard. For it remains the case that there is a difference between God and the world, the 'element of asymmetry' which John Macquarrie emphasizes. This difference can be overstated, with the consequences already noted, but it should not be ignored. However, we have already seen that this element of asymmetry is compatible with the model of the universe as God's body, understood analogously to persons and their bodies. There is one sense in which it is mistaken to say that a person is more than his or her body; there is another sense in which it is true. In its true sense it is a recognition that personhood cannot be defined reductionistically in terms of embodiment, rather than embodiment in terms of personhood. In its false sense, it is an attempt to divide persons into disparate pieces, a body piece and a soul piece, conjoined and interacting in some mysterious way. Similarly, if the world is God's body, there is a sense in which it is true to say that God and the world are a single reality; there is not a 'spiritual substance' over against the world. But this does not mean that God is reducible to mechanism and physical statistics any more than personhood is reducible to physiological data. If pantheism is reductionism, it is unacceptable. But the claim that the universe is God's body in the sense I have described does not entail that variety of pantheism, and is compatible with the doctrine of divine transcendence analogous to the way human embodiment is compatible with human transcendence.

3. The Many

Once we recognize the truth to which pantheism points, however, a new question is bound to arise. If ultimately there is only one reality, not two, if there is nothing irreducibly other than God, then how can there be genuine individuality and autonomy? If the universe is God's body, and we are part of the universe, then we are part of God's body. But how then can we still be ourselves – persons with freedom? It will not do to suggest that the individual members of God's body are not subject to his absolute control, on the analogy of the way many organs of our bodies are not controllable by taking thought, because I have already argued that it is precisely here that the model must be qualified. God is, in the sense specified, more completely embodied than we are; that is, in virtue of his omnipotence and omniscience he is in immediate awareness and control of every aspect of the universe. In more traditional terms, even such freedom as we have, we have only by the continued gift of God, and our autonomy is subject to his sovereignty. But then how is autonomy possible at all?

It is usually assumed – and I share the assumption – that unless there is indeed human autonomy then moral and religious life is impossible. Love cannot be commanded; and although love at a human level should perhaps be described as responsive love rather than initiatory love, even the response must be free, not manipulated. Without love, Christianity is empty. But if we are all part of God, and in his direct control at every moment, how can we be free to love? This indeed is one of the legitimate reasons why pantheism is sometimes feared, for if it collapses the distinctions between God and creatures it forfeits their independent existence.

The doctrine of creation, after all, is two-sided. On the one hand it does affirm that all reality is from God; nothing has a prior or independent existence. In this sense creation points towards pantheism, as discussed above. But on the other hand it points to the creation of independent individuals – heavenly bodies, plants, animals, persons – who do exist in some sense over against God. Their independence may be a derived independence, but it is independence nonetheless. The biblical story of Adam naming the animals pictures this in a dramatic way: the animals were created by God, true, and owed their origin and continuation to him, but they were separate individuals, different from God and from one another, and could thus be name-bearers, creatures existing in their own right and with their own identities. How can this be compatible with a model of the universe as God's body?

The first thing to be said in response is that this is not, contrary to appearances, a special problem for this model which would not arise for cosmic dualism. Unless cosmic dualism is taken to such an extreme that the world and the things in it have an origin and an existence utterly independent of God (in which case it has surrendered its claim to be a Christian position) the problem of how there can be individuality and autonomy if God is sovereign creator and sustainer must arise. Whether the theist thinks of God and the world as one reality or not, whatever reality he ascribes to the world must be derived reality, not intrinsic, and the problem still arises: how can there be genuine autonomy if God is sovereign?

Just as the problem of evil, though a real problem, is not increased by seeing the world as the embodiment of God, so also the problem of human freedom, though begging for a solution, is no more acute if the universe is God's body than if it is something separate from him of which he has complete immediate knowledge and over which he exercises omnipotent control.

Accordingly, I shall do no more here than sketch an outline of a solution which would, I believe, comport well with the idea of the universe as the embodiment of God. The first point to notice is that as long as we concentrate on doctrines of divine omnipotence and divine infinity we are unlikely to arrive at any answers. It is only if these are somehow limited that there can be any thought of individuality and autonomy of things other than God. Now, there is no force outside of God which could limit him if he is omnipotent, and therefore concentrating on divine power will for the purposes of this problem get us nowhere.

But it is not a new thing for theologians to be so preoccupied with God's 'omni-attributes' that they forget that the first thing the Bible says about God is that he is Creator, and that the most emphatic and significant thing it says is that he is love. If Jesus of Nazareth rather than Aristotle's Unmoved Mover is central to our concept of God, then the proper order of priority in understanding the attributes of God must be to take his love as central, and modify our ideas of omnipotence, omniscience, and so on, in terms of it, rather than the other way around. But creative love is love which gives autonomy to that which it creates; and though omnipotence can be limited by nothing else, it is limited by love. God could, of course, override all our individuality and freedom – could, that is, if he ceased to love. But love places restraints on power. Love gives, power takes away. If God's power is understood as the expression of his love, however, then God's power is his power to give independence, autonomy, even to creatures over whom, strictly speaking, he is sovereign. His power is thus not merely power over weak and fragile creatures, but power over himself, the strength of self-restraint, giving reality to individual creatures and fostering rather than inhibiting their autonomy. In John Macquarrie's phrase, 'Being itself lets be the beings', brings them into being and fosters their independence, even though apart from him they are nothing.

Too often, the picture of God has been of one who presided over his creation, giving, but without cost to himself, with predetermined triumph already assured. But if a friend, a parent, or a spouse treated us with this uncosting condescension and called it love we could only be scornful. If God's love to us is more than a phrase, it costs him something, a limiting of himself, an expenditure of his power on behalf of our autonomy, not against it. Indeed, the model of the universe as God's embodiment provides a good way of thinking about God which sees his love as central, pouring himself out for individuals, with no limits on his self-giving. He is the One who is All, yet to whom the Many owe their freedom and their very selves.

> The infinity of the universe must be understood, with awe, as the expression of the consequence of the limitlessness of the divine self-giving: for the divine aspiration to give must ever enlarge the bounds of that which is to receive. Nothing must be withheld from the self-giving which is creation: no unexpended resources of divine power or potentiality: no 'glory of God' or 'majesty of God' which may be compared and contrasted with the glory of the galaxies and the majesty of the universe: no 'eternity of God' which might outlive an eternal universe. It is to be understood that the universe is not to be equated with 'that which science knows', nor even with 'that which science might, in principle, come to know': the universe is the totality of being for which God gives himself in love.[13]

In the last section we noticed that God is frequently spoken of as Being Itself, not a being among beings, and we saw the point of this. But it is only half a truth. If God loves, then he pours himself out for the autonomous existence of individuals, and in that sense is a person to whom other persons can respond, a being among beings. He does not compel or manipulate but invites response. By creating individuals and inviting their love, he has limited himself to the status of a being, an individual, over against them. This would be a very misleading half of the truth if the other half were not also remembered: that, as creator and sustainer, no creature exists or has autonomy except from him: God is All, Being Itself. One-sided emphasis on human autonomy impoverishes our appreciation of God's sovereignty. Yet one-sided emphasis on his sovereignty can easily hide from us the extent of his self-giving love, in whom we, finite and dependent and yet autonomous, live and move and have our being. The two sides complement one another in an understanding of God's creative love, and are consistent with the model of the universe as God's body, a body some of whose parts

13. W. H. Vanstone *Love's Endeavour, Love's Expense* pp. 59–60.

have been given a measure of autonomy in God's gracious self-manifestation. 'Now ye are the body of Christ, and members in particular.'

Postscript

Cartesian dualism, the notion that persons are composed of two parts, a body and a soul, which could in principle be sundered, has been with us for several centuries, and can still claim advocates though it is no longer at the centre of philosophical fashion. Apart from showing that Cartesian dualism raises certain problems for traditional theology, I have not advanced detailed arguments against it. Clearly the bare fact that it is now unfashionable is not an argument against its truth; and those who continue to find it a convincing account of human persons will not find this essay a serious challenge to their position.

Nevertheless, many people today, whether trained in philosophy or not, no longer find Cartesian dualism a plausible picture of human personhood: I share this view, though I have not argued for it. Yet the traditional picture of God and the universe as two separate realities, one spiritual and the other material, is simply dualism on a cosmic scale. Those who find dualism an untenable account of human persons may well be dismayed if they find that theism nevertheless requires them to accept it as an account of God and the world: in fact they may, like Kai Nielsen, think that this is sufficient reason for rejecting theism as incoherent.[1] So we have set about the task of inquiring what the consequences would be if the move from dualism to holism, now made in a discussion of human personhood, were also made on a cosmic level within the framework of Christian theology. And I have suggested that, just as this move has liberating effects for our understanding of human persons, so also it illuminates many of the attributes predicated of God.

In the thinking of the Fathers, three main streams fed the doctrine of divine incorporeality: metaphysics, morality and mysticism. Each of these, I suggest, is also affected by a shift from a dualistic to a holistic picture of God and the world; and the effect in each case is wholesome. In the case of metaphysics, this is obvious. Any theist

---

1. This is clearly one of the undercurrents in Kai Nielsen's *Scepticism*, for instance.

who finds metaphysical dualism inadequate as an account of human persons cannot help but feel his or her integrity undermined if he or she must nevertheless affirm it at a cosmic level. If we take seriously the recent philosophical discussions of incorporeal perception and agency, we must either find some way to refute the conclusion that disembodied personhood is an incoherent notion – in my view an unpromising enterprise – or else succumb to an uncomfortable and disreputable double-think. The shift of perspective from cosmic dualism to the affirmation that God and the world are a single reality makes this embarrassing metaphysical shuffle unnecessary. It also answers those who reject theism on the grounds of the incoherence of incorporeal personhood. And the re-evaluation of the traditional attributes of God and the clarifying of our concepts about him which this perspective calls forth is in itself illuminating and worth while.

In terms of morality, the results are again productive. Any view which sets God and the world in contrast to one another carries the (psychological if not logical) consequence that we feel obliged to 'choose sides'. The annals of medieval church history are full of the consequences of choosing God over against the world: this had the effect of making the world, including human bodies, alien, to be regarded as material objects to be dominated, repressed or manipulated, but hardly understood or communed with. If the medievals tended to choose God rather than the world, post-Enlightenment civilization in the west makes the opposite choice and leaves God outside the secular universe, to be ignored for all practical purposes. Thus an unbridled asceticism and an unbridled lust for technological power spring from the same root: a rift between the material world and spiritual value.

Not that this would be a necessary consequence of traditional theology. On the contrary, a proper emphasis on a doctrine of creation and a world which God pronounces good will go a long way, even within a traditional framework, towards seeing ourselves and the world as God's valuable self-manifestation, especially when this is reinforced by a doctrine of incarnation and sacramental theology and practice. But it is difficult to sustain this strong view of divine immanence and the value of creation in juxtaposition with a traditional contrast between God and the world; and so the shuffle begins again. The model of the universe as God's body helps to do justice to the beauty and value of nature, the importance of conservation and ecological responsibility, the significance and dignity of the human body and human sexuality.

156

Earth's crammed with heaven
And every common bush on fire with God;
But only those who see take off their shoes . . .
The rest sit round it and pluck blackberries,
And daub their natural faces unawares . . . [2]

Those who have once seen themselves, and the world about them, as the embodiment and self-manifestation of God are unlikely to continue to treat it in a cavalier way or feel it utterly alien or devoid of intrinsic significance and worth.

And what of mysticism – both the peaks of spiritual experiences of Mother Julian and Meister Eckhart, and the more prosaic religious experiences that vitalize the belief and practice of men and women around the world? The doctrines of divine immanence and omnipresence essential to religious experience are congenial to the model of the universe as the embodiment of God. Clearly also this model injects new life into an understanding of the sacraments, especially the Eucharist, which for many Christians is the focus of spirituality. But it may be that more can be said, and in conclusion I offer the following tentative suggestion.

Writers on mysticism and spirituality have often made a distinction between nature (or extrovertive) mysticism and spiritual (or introvertive) mysticism, and a further distinction between those who claim that at the peak of mystical experience all is One – they are wholly united with God – and those who maintain that there is still, even at this level, an essential distinction between Creator and creature. There is then discussion about which of these is 'true' mysticism, which is 'highest': it has been seriously argued that nature mysticism is a lower form, while true inwardness is the essence of spirituality, and also that any doctrine claiming essential oneness (as for instance Meister Eckhart's) is heretical.[3]

Now, if God and the universe are one reality, not two, and if at the height of spiritual experience mystics are granted an encounter with God more intimate than most people ever experience, all of these distinctions can perhaps be understood and reconciled. In the first place, nature mysticism – an existential awareness of God in the universe or some aspect of it – is understandable; so also, however, is the introvertive experience of divine transcendence, for it could be experienced both as the inner unity of the person with

2. Elizabeth Barrett Browning *Aurora Leigh.*
3. Cf. R.C. Zaehner *Mysticism Sacred and Profane;* W.T. Stace *Mysticism and Philosophy;* W.R. Inge *Christian Mysticism.*

God, and as the awareness that this reality of the self and God are not *reducible* to the physical world. Perhaps mystics encounter in personal existential terms that which my theory attempts to articulate intellectually. The point is, there is no need, if I am correct, to engage in what must be a most repugnant task, namely to argue that one variety of religious experience is to be discredited while another is 'higher' or 'truer'. Yet neither is there any need to force all religious experience into the same mould contrary to all appearances.

Similarly for the distinction between Oneness and plurality: the mystic who says with Eckhart that 'the eye with which I see God is the eye with which God sees me', may be encountering at an intense existential level the truth that God is All, that our reality as human persons is part of the reality of God. His fellow mystic, who insists that even at the height of mystical union there is still a distinction between himself and God, is perhaps finding in his encounter that although on the one hand God is All, God's loving self-limitation calls forth authentically autonomous individuals who are not collapsed into his totality. If this suggestion approaches the truth, it would apply in the same way to more ordinary religious experience as well, where the same sorts of distinctions between looking inward and outward, feelings of the unity of the self and God and feelings of God as the numinous Other abound. There need then be no sense of conflict between these varieties.

And might it also help to bridge the gap between the religious experiences of different world religions? If this would turn out to be true – and it would need to be investigated very carefully – then the implications for mysticism and religious experience might be the most fruitful consequence of an adoption of the doctrine of the universe as the embodiment of God.

Bibliography

Abbreviations

1. Biblical
   AV: Authorized Version.
   NEB: New English Bible.
   RSV: Revised Standard Version.

2. Other
   ANCL: *Ante-Nicene Christian Library* (T. and T. Clark, Edinburgh, and Wm. B. Eerdmans, Grand Rapids, Michigan) 1864f.
   DK: Diels, Hermann and Kranz, Walther *Die Fragmente der Vorsocratiker* 10th ed. (Berlin) 1960. I have normally followed the translation provided by Kirk, G.S. and Raven, J.E. *The Presocratic Philosophers* (Cambridge University Press, London and New York) 1957.
   FC: *The Fathers of the Church* (Catholic University of America Press, Washington, D.C.) 1947f.
   GCS: *Die griechischen christlichen Schriftsteller der ersten drei Jahrhunderte* (Leipzig and Berlin) 1897f.
   LCC: *Library of Christian Classics* (SCM, London) 1954f.
   LF: *Library of the Fathers* (Parker, Oxford, and Rivington, London) 1850f.
   LOEB: *Loeb Classical Library* (William Heinemann, London, and Harvard University Press, Cambridge, Mass.) 1912f.
   M: Migne, J.P. *Patrologia Graeca* (Paris) 1857–66.
   NPNF: *A Select Library of Nicene and Post-Nicene Fathers* (Oxford University Press, Oxford) 1890f.

Articles

Brain, Lord 'Some Aspects of the Brain–Mind Relationship' in Smythies, J.R., ed. *Brain and Mind* (Routledge, London, and Humanities Press, New York) 1965.

159

Cullmann, Oscar 'Immortality of the Soul or Resurrection of the Dead?' in Stendahl, Krister, ed. *Immortality and Resurrection* (Macmillan, New York) 1965.

Danto, Arthur 'Basic Actions' in *American Philosophical Quarterly* Vol. 2, 1965.

Dennett, Daniel 'Conditions of Personhood' in Rorty, Amélie O., ed. *The Identities of Persons* (University of California Press, Berkeley) 1976.

Dominian, Jack 'Psychology of Prayer I' in his *Cycles of Affirmation* (Darton, Longman and Todd, London) 1975.

Flew, Antony 'Is There a Case for Disembodied Survival?' in *The Journal of the American Society for Psychical Research* Vol. 66 No. 2, 1972.

Flew, Antony 'Some Objections to Cartesian Views of Man' in Smythies, J.R., ed. *Brain and Mind* (Routledge, London, and Humanities Press, New York) 1965.

Geach, Peter 'What do we Think With?' in his *God and the Soul* (Routledge, London, and Schocken, New York) 1969.

Hallie, Philip 'Stoicism' in Edwards, Paul, ed. *The Encyclopedia of Philosophy* Vol. 8 (Macmillan and Free Press, New York, and Macmillan, London) 1967.

Harrison, Jonathon 'The Embodiment of Mind Or What Use Is Having a Body?' in *Proceedings of the Aristotelian Society* 1973–4.

Hebblethwaite, Brian L. 'Providence and Divine Action' in *Religious Studies* Vol. 14, 1978.

Helm, Paul 'God and Spacelessness' in *Philosophy* Vol. 55 No. 212, April, 1980.

Henry, Paul 'The Place of Plotinus in the History of Thought' in Plotinus *Enneads* (E.T. S. MacKenna, 3rd ed., Faber & Faber, London) 1962.

Hunt, W. Murray 'Some Remarks About the Embodiment of God' in *Religious Studies* Vol. 17, 1981.

Jantzen, Grace M. 'Miracles, History and Apologetics' in *Christian Scholar's Review* Vol. VIII No. 4, 1979.

Jantzen, Grace M. 'Miracles Reconsidered' in *Christian Scholar's Review* Vol. IX No. 4, 1980.

Jantzen, Grace M. 'On Worshipping an Embodied God' in *Canadian Journal of Philosophy* Vol. III No. 3, 1978.

Jantzen (Dyck), Grace M. 'Omnipresence and Incorporeality' in *Religious Studies* Vol. 13, 1977.

Kneale, William 'Time and Eternity in Theology' in *Proceedings of the Aristotelian Society* 1960–61.

Lessing, G.E. 'On the Reality of Things Outside God' in Chadwick, Henry, ed. *Lessing's Theological Writings* (A. and C. Black, London) 1956.

Lossky, Vladimir 'Redemption and Deification' in his *In the Image and Likeness of God* (E.T. Mowbrays, London) 1975.

Mabbott, J.D. 'Our Direct Experience of Time' in *Mind* Vol. LX, 1951.

Macquarrie, John 'God and the World: One Reality or Two?' in *Theology* Vol. LXXV No. 626, 1972.

McMullin, Ernan 'The Concept of Matter' in his (ed.) *The Concept of Matter in Greek and Medieval Philosophy* (University of Notre Dame Press, Notre Dame, Ind.) 1963.

Merlan, P. 'Greek Philosophy from Plato to Plotinus' in Armstrong, A.H., ed. *The Cambridge History of Later Greek and Early Medieval Philosophy* (Cambridge University Press, London and New York) 1967.

Minkowski, H. 'Space and Time' in Smart, J.J.C., ed. *Problems of Space and Time* (Macmillan, New York) 1964.

Muilenberg, James 'Is There a Biblical Theology?' in *Union Seminary Quarterly Review* Vol. XII No. 4.

Mundle, C.W.K. 'Time, Consciousness of' in Edwards, Paul, ed. *The Encyclopedia of Philosophy* Vol. 8 (Macmillan and Free Press, New York and Macmillan, London) 1967.

Mundle, C.W.K. 'How Specious is the Specious Present?' in *Mind* Vol. LXIII, 1954.

Quine, W.V.O. 'On What There Is' in his *From a Logical Point of View* 2nd ed. (Harper and Row, New York) 1963.

Rorty, Amélie O. 'A Literary Postscript' in her (ed.) *The Identities of Persons* (University of California Press, Berkeley) 1976.

Smart, J.J.C. 'Time' in Edwards, Paul, ed. *The Encyclopedia of Philosophy* Vol. 8 (Macmillan and Free Press, New York and Macmillan, London) 1967.

Sutherland, Stewart R. 'God, Time and Eternity' in *Proceedings of the Aristotelian Society* 1979.

Swinburne, Richard 'The Argument from Design – a Defence' in *Religious Studies* Vol. 8, 1972.

Swinburne, Richard 'Personal Identity' in *Proceedings of the Aristotelian Society* 1973–4.

Swinburne, Richard 'Persons and Personal Identity' in Lewis, H.D., ed. *Contemporary British Philosophy* Fourth Series (George Allen & Unwin, London) 1976.

Theodore of Mopsuestia 'On the Incarnation VII' in Wiles, M. and

Santer, M., eds. *Documents in Early Christian Thought* (Cambridge University Press, Cambridge and New York) 1975.

Whitrow, G.J. 'Einstein' in Edwards, Paul, ed. *The Encyclopedia of Philosophy* Vol. 2 (Macmillan and Free Press, New York, and Macmillan, London) 1967.

Wiles, Maurice 'Religious Authority and Divine Action' in *Religious Studies* Vol. 7, 1971.

Williams, Bernard 'Persons, Character and Morality' in Rorty, Amélie O., ed. *The Identities of Persons* (University of California Press, Berkeley) 1976.

Young, Frances 'The God of the Greeks' in Schoedel, William R. and Wilken, Robert L., eds. *Early Christian Literature and the Classical Intellectual Traditions:* in Honorem Robert M. Grant Théologie Historique 53 (Beauchesne) 1979.

Books

Alexander, H.G., ed. *The Leibniz-Clarke Correspondence* (Manchester University Press, Manchester) 1956.

Alexander, S. *Space, Time and Deity* Vols. I and II, Gifford Lectures for 1916–18 (Macmillan, London) 1927.

Allen, R.E. *Plato's 'Euthyphro' and the Earlier Theory of Forms* (Routledge, London) 1970.

Anselm *Basic Writings* (E.T. S.N. Deane, Open Court, La Salle, Ill.) 1962.

Aristotle *The Basic Works* (E.T. Richard McKeon, ed. Random House, New York) 1941.

Armstrong, A.H. *The Architecture of the Intelligible Universe in the Philosophy of Plotinus* (Cambridge University Press, London and New York) 1940.

Armstrong, A.H., ed. *The Cambridge History of Later Greek and Early Medieval Philosophy* (Cambridge University Press, London and New York) 1967.

Armstrong, D.M. *A Materialist Theory of the Mind* (Routledge, London, and Humanities Press, New York) 1968.

Athanasius *Defence of the Nicene Definition* NPNF Vol. IV.

Athanasius *On the Incarnation* (E.T. R.W. Thomson, Clarendon, Oxford) 1971.

Attenborough, David *Life on Earth* (Collins, London and New York) 1979.

Augustine of Hippo *City of God* (E.T. Henry Bettenson, Penguin, Harmondsworth, Middlesex) 1972.

Augustine of Hippo *Commentary on the Gospel of John* LF Vol. 26.

Augustine of Hippo *Confessions* (E.T. John K. Ryan, Image Books, Doubleday, New York and Mayflower, London) 1960.

Augustine of Hippo *The Trinity* LCC Vol. VIII.

Badham, Paul *The Christian Doctrine of Life After Death* (Macmillan, London, and Barnes and Noble, New York) 1976.

Barr, James *Biblical Words for Time* 2nd ed. (SCM, London, and Allenson, Naperville, Ill.) 1969.

Barth, Karl *Church Dogmatics* Vols. 1–3 (E.T. T. & T. Clarke, Edinburgh) 1936–75.

Barth, Karl *The Epistle to the Romans* (E.T. of the 1922 German edition, Oxford University Press, Oxford and New York) 1933.

Barth, Karl *The Humanity of God* (E.T. Collins, London, and John Knox Press, Altanta, Ga.) 1960/1961.

Bergson, Henri *Time and Free Will* (E.T. Swan Sonnenshein & Co., London) 1910.

Bigg, C. *The Christian Platonists of Alexandria* (Oxford University Press, Oxford) 1886.

Boehme, Jakob *The Way to Christ* (E.T. Peter Erb, Paulist Press, New York, and SPCK, London) 1978.

Boethius *The Consolation of Philosophy* (E.T. Richard Green, Liberal Arts Press, New York) 1962.

Bradley, F.H. *Appearance and Reality* 2nd. ed. (Clarendon, Oxford and Macmillan, New York) 1897/1902.

Brooke, Rupert *Poems of Rupert Brooke* (Geoffrey Keynes, ed., Thomas Nelson & Sons, London) 1952.

Browning, Elizabeth Barrett *Aurora Leigh and Other Poems* (Women's Press, London, and J. Miller, New York) 1978.

Buber, Martin *I and Thou* (E.T. Walter Kaufmann, T. and T. Clark, Edinburgh, and Charles Scribner's Sons, New York) 1970.

Bultmann, Rudolf *The Gospel of John* (E.T. Basil Blackwell, Oxford, and Westminster Press, Philadelphia) 1971.

Bultmann, Rudolf *Theology of the New Testament* Vols. I and II (E.T. SCM, London, and Charles Scribner's Sons, New York) 1952.

Caird, John *The Fundamental Ideas of Christianity* Vols. I and II Gifford Lectures for 1895–6 (MacLehose and Sons, Glasgow) 1899.

Cherniss, H.F. *The Riddle of the Early Academy* (University of California Press, Berkeley and Los Angeles) 1945.

Clement of Alexandria *Exhortation to the Greeks* LOEB.

Clement of Alexandria *Fragment from the Book of Providence* ANCL Vol. 24.

Clement of Alexandria *Stromaties* NPNF Vol. IV.

Cloud of Unknowing (E.T. Clifton Wolters, Penguin, Harmondsworth, Middlesex) 1961.

Copleston, F. *The History of Philosophy* Vols. 1–9 (Search Press, London, and Image Books, Doubleday, New York) 1962–77.

Cornford, F.M. *Plato's Cosmology* (Routledge, London and Humanties Press, New York) 1937.

Cornford, F.M. *Plato's Theory of Knowledge* (Kegan Paul & Co., London) 1935.

Crombie, I.M. *An Examination of Plato's Doctrines:* Vol. 1 *Plato on Man and Society;* Vol. 2 *Plato on Knowledge and Reality* (Routledge, London, and Humanities Press, New York) 1963.

Cullmann, Oscar *Christ and Time* 2nd ed. (E.T. SCM, London) 1962.

Dampier, W.C. *A History of Science* 4th ed. (Cambridge University Press, London and New York) 1966.

Dionysius the Areopagite *The Mystical Theology* (E.T. C.E. Rolt, SPCK, London) 1940.

Edwards, Paul, ed. *The Encyclopedia of Philosophy* Vols. 1–8 (Macmillan and Free Press, New York, and Macmillan, London) 1967.

Eichrodt, Walter *Theology of the Old Testament* Vols. I & II (E.T. SCM, London, and Westminster Press, Philadelphia) 1967.

Einstein, A., *et al. The Principle of Relativity* (Methuen, London and New York) 1923.

Eusebius *The Oration of Eusebius in Praise of Constantine* NPNF Vol. 1.

Feigl, Herbert *The 'Mental' and the 'Physical'* (University of Minnesota Press, Minneapolis) 1967 and OUP 1968.

Flew, Antony *God and Philosophy* (Harcourt, New York, Hutchinson, London) 1966.

Flew, R.N. *The Idea of Perfection in Christian Theology* (Oxford University Press, Oxford and New York) 1934.

Garrigou-Lagrange, R. *God: His Existence and Nature: A Thomistic Solution to Certain Agnostic Antinomies* Vols. I and II (E.T. Herder, London, and St Louis, Mo.) 1934.

Geach, Peter *God and the Soul* (Routledge, London, and Schocken, New York) 1969.

Gilsen, Étienne *The Christian Philosophy of St Thomas Aquinas* (E.T. Victor Gollancz, London) 1957.

Goheen, John *The Problem of Matter and Form in the De Ente et Essentia of Thomas Aquinas* (Harvard University Press, Cambridge, Mass.) 1940.

Gregory of Nazianzus *Oration* NPNF Vol. VII.

Gregory of Nazianzus *Second Theological Oration* NPNF Vol. VII.

Gregory of Nyssa *Against Eunomius* NPNF Vol. V.

Gregory of Nyssa *Catechetical Oration* (E.T. J.H. Srawley, Cambridge University Press, Cambridge) 1903.

Gregory of Nyssa *On the Soul and the Resurrection* (De Anima et Resurrectione) M 46.12.

Gunton, Colin *Becoming and Being: The Doctrine of God in Charles Hartshorne and Karl Barth* (Oxford University Press, Oxford and New York) 1978.

Hampshire, Stuart *Spinoza* (Penguin, Harmondsworth, Middlesex) 1951.

Harnack, Adolf *History of Dogma* Vols. 1–7 (E.T. Peter Smith, Gloucester, Mass.) 1976.

Harré, Rom *The Principles of Scientific Thinking* (Macmillan, London, and University of Chicago Press) 1970.

Hartshorne, Charles *The Divine Relativity: A Social Conception of God* (Yale University Press, New Haven) 1948.

Hegel, G.W.F. *Logic* (E.T. William Wallace, Clarendon, Oxford) 1978.

Hegel G.W.F. *Phenomenology of Spirit* (E.T. A.V. Miller, Clarendon, Oxford) 1979.

Hegel, G.W.F. *The Spirit of Christianity; Early Theological Writings* (E.T. T.M. Knox, University of Chicago Press) 1948.

Hick, John *Arguments for the Existence of God* (Macmillan, London, and Seabury, New York) 1971.

Hick, John *Death and Eternal Life* (Collins, London) 1976.

Hippolytus of Rome *Refutation of Heresies* ANCL Vol. VI.

Husserl, Edmund *The Phenomenology of Internal Time Consciousness* (E.T. Indiana University Press, Bloomington, Indiana) 1964.

Illingworth, J.R. *Divine Immanence: An Essay on the Spiritual Significance of Matter* (Macmillan, London) 1898.

Inge, W.R. *Christian Mysticism* Bampton Lectures for 1899 (Methuen, London) 1899.

Irenaeus *Against Heresies* LF Vol. 42.

James, William *Principles of Psychology* Vols. I and II (Macmillan, London, and H. Holt, New York) 1890.

James, William *The Varieties of Religious Experience* Gifford Lectures for 1901–2 (Fontana, Collins, London and Image Books, Doubleday, New York) 1977.

John Chrysostom *Homilies in John* FC Vol. 41.

John of Damascus *The Orthodox Faith* FC Vol. 37.

Justin Martyr *Apology* ANCL Vol. 2.

Justin Martyr *Dialogue with Trypho* ANCL Vol. 2.

Justin Martyr *Hortatory Address to the Greeks* ANCL Vol. 1.

Kant, Immanuel *Critique of Judgement* (E.T. J.C. Meredith, Oxford University Press, Oxford) 1928.

Kant, Immanuel *Critique of Pure Reason* (E.T. Norman Kemp Smith, Macmillan, Londoh) 1929.

Kant, Immanuel *Religion within the Limits of Reason Alone* (E.T. Theodore M. Greene and Hoyt H. Hudson, with an Introductory Essay by John R. Silber, Hamish Hamilton, London, and Harper and Row, New York) 1960.

Katz, Steven T., ed. *Mysticism and Philosophical Analysis* (Sheldon Press, London) 1978.

Kaufmann, Gordon *God the Problem* (Harvard University Press, Cambridge, Mass.) 1972.

Kelly, J.N.D. *Early Christian Doctrines* 2nd ed. (A. and C. Black, London, and Harper and Row, New York) 1960.

Kenny, Anthony *The Five Ways* (Routledge, London and Schocken, New York) 1969.

Kenny, Anthony *The God of the Philosophers* (Clarendon, Oxford and New York) 1979.

Kittel, Gerhard, ed. *Theological Dictionary of the New Testament* (E.T. G.W. Bromiley, Wm. B. Eerdmans, Grand Rapids, Mich.) 1969.

Lampe, G.W.H., ed. *A Patristic Greek Lexicon* (Clarendon, Oxford and New York) 1961.

Lampe, G.W.H. *God as Spirit* Bampton Lectures for 1976 (Clarendon, Oxford) 1977.

Lewis, H.D. *The Elusive Mind* Gifford Lectures for 1966–68 (George Allen and Unwin, London) 1969.

Locke, John *An Enquiry Concerning Human Understanding* (Peter H. Nidditch, ed. Oxford University Press, Oxford) 1975.

Lovejoy, Arthur *The Great Chain of Being* (Harvard University Press, Cambridge, Mass.) 1957.

Lucas, J.R. *A Treatise on Time and Space* (Methuen, London and New York) 1973.

Macquarrie, John *Principles of Christian Theology* 2nd ed. (SCM, London) 1977.

McMullin, Ernan, ed. *The Concept of Matter in Greek and Medieval Philosophy* (University of Notre Dame Press, Notre Dame, Ind.) 1963.

McNabb, Vincent, ed. *The Decrees of the Vatican Council* (London) 1907.

Merton, Thomas *Seeds of Contemplation* (Anthony Clarke Books, Wheathampstead, Hertfordshire) 1961.

Methodius of Olympus *Discourse on the Resurrection* and *On Free Will* ANCL Vol. XIV.

Miles, Margaret R. *Augustine on the Body* AAR Dissertation Series 31 (Scholar's Press, Missoula, Mont.) 1979.

Moltmann, Jürgen *Theology of Hope* (E.T. SCM, London) 1967.

Newton, Sir Isaac *Mathematical Principles of Natural Philosophy* (E.T. Florian Cajori, University of California Press, Berkeley) 1934.

Niebuhr, Reinhold *The Nature and Destiny of Man* Vols. I and II (Nisbet and Co., London and New York) 1941.

Nielsen, Kai *Scepticism* (Macmillan, London and St Martins' Press, New York) 1973.

Ogden, Schubert *The Reality of God* 2nd ed. (Harper and Row, New York and London) 1977.

Origen *Against Celsus* (E.T. Henry Chadwick, Cambridge University Press, Cambridge and New York) 1953.

Origen *Commentary on the Gospel of John* GCS Vol. 10.

Origen *On First Principles* ANCL Vol. X.

Owen, H.P. *Concepts of Deity* (Macmillan, London and Seabury, New York) 1971.

Peacocke, Arthur, R. *Creation and the World of Science* Bampton Lectures for 1978 (Clarendon, Oxford and New York) 1979.

Pelikan, Jaroslav *The Christian Tradition* Vol. 1: *The Emergence of the Catholic Tradition (100–600)* (University of Chicago Press) 1971.

Penelhum, Terence *Survival and Disembodied Existence* (Routledge, London and New York) 1970.

Pike, Nelson *God and Timelessness* (Routledge, London and New York) 1970.

Plato *Collected Dialogues* (E.T. Edith Hamilton and Huntington Cairns, eds. Princeton University Press, New Jersey) 1963.

Plotinus *Enneads* (E.T. Nos. I-III LOEB; Nos. IV-VI S. MacKenna, 3rd ed. Faber & Faber, London) 1962. For Nos. IV-VI I have also had the benefit of A.H. Armstrong's translations, forthcoming in LOEB.

Popper, Sir Karl R. and Eccles, Sir John C. *The Self and its Brain* (Springer International, London and New York) 1977.

Prestige, G.L. *God in Patristic Thought* (SPCK, London) 1952.

Pringle-Pattison, A. Seth *The Idea of God in the Light of Recent Philo-*

sophy Gifford Lectures for 1912–13 (Oxford University Press, Oxford and New York) 1917/1920.

Quinton, Anthony *The Nature of Things* (Routledge, London and Boston) 1973.

Rahner, Karl *Foundations of Christian Faith* (E.T. Darton, Longman and Todd, London) 1978.

Rist, J.M. *Plotinus* (Cambridge University Press, Cambridge and New York) 1967.

Rist, J.M. *Stoic Philosophy* (Cambridge University Press, Cambridge and New York) 1969.

Rorty, Amélie O., ed. *The Identities of Persons* (University of California Press, Berkeley) 1976.

Ross, W.D. *Aristotle* (Methuen, London) 1930.

Schleiermacher, F. *The Christian Faith* (E.T. T. & T. Clark, Edinburgh) 1928.

Schlick, Moritz *The Philosophy of Nature* (E.T. Amethe von Zeppelin, Philosophical Library, New York) 1949.

Shoemaker, Sydney *Self-Knowledge and Self-Identity* (Cornell University Press, Ithaca, New York) 1963.

Sklar, Lawrence *Space, Time and Spacetime* (University of California Press, Berkeley) 1974.

Smart, J.J.C., ed. *Problems of Space and Time* (Macmillan, New York and London) 1964.

Smythies, J.R., ed. *Brain and Mind: Modern Concepts of the Nature of Mind* (Routledge, London, and Humanities Press, New York) 1965.

Spinoza, B. *Ethics* (E.T. R.H.M. Elwes, Dover, New York) 1955.

Stace, W.T. *Mysticism and Philosophy* (Macmillan, London) 1961.

Stendahl, Krister, ed. *Immortality and Resurrection* (Macmillan, New York) 1965.

Stoudt, John Joseph *Sunrise to Eternity* (University of Philadelphia Press) 1957.

Sutherland, Stewart *Atheism and the Rejection of God* (Basil Blackwell, Oxford) 1977.

Swinburne, Richard *The Coherence of Theism* (Clarendon, Oxford and New York) 1977.

Swinburne, Richard *The Existence of God* (Clarendon, Oxford and New York) 1979.

Tatian *Oration to the Greeks* ANCL Vol. III.

Taylor, Charles *Hegel* (Cambridge University Press, Cambridge and New York) 1975.

Tertullian *Against Praxeas* ANCL Vol. XV.

Theodoret of Cyprus *The Dialogues* (Critical edition Gerard H. Ettlinger, Clarendon, Oxford) 1975.

Thomas Aquinas *Commentary on Aristotle's 'Physics'* (E.T. R.J. Blackwell *et al.*, Yale University Press, New Haven) 1963.

Thomas Aquinas *Commentary on the Metaphysics of Aristotle* (E.T. J.P. Rowan, Regnery, Chicago) 1961.

Thomas Aquinas *On Being and Essence* (E.T. Armand Maurer, 2nd ed. Pontifical Institute of Mediaeval Studies, Toronto) 1968.

Thomas Aquinas *Summa Contra Gentiles* Books I-IV (E.T. Anton C. Pegis, University of Notre Dame Press, Notre Dame, Ill.) 1975.

Thomas Aquinas *Summa Theologiae* (E.T. Blackfriars, London) 1964f.

Thornton, Martin *Prayer: A New Encounter* (SPCK, London) 1972.

Tillich, Paul *Dynamics of Faith* (Harper and Row, New York and London) 1956.

Tillich, Paul *Systematic Theology* Vols. I-III (SCM, London and University of Chicago Press) 1963.

Van Frassen, Bas C. *An Introduction to the Philosophy of Time and Space* (Random House, New York) 1970.

Vanstone, W.H. *Love's Endeavour, Love's Expense* (Darton, Longman and Todd, London) 1977.

Virgil *Aeneid* (E.T. John Dryden, Macmillan, London, and Airmont Publishing Co., New York) 1965/1968.

Von Hügel, Baron F. *The Mystical Element of Religion* Vols. I and II (J.M. Dent, London, and Dutton, New York) 1908.

Von Rad, Gerhard *Old Testament Theology* Vols. I and II (E.T. SCM, London) 1975.

Watts, Alan *Behold the Spirit* 2nd. ed. (Vintage Books, Random House, New York) 1971.

Whitrow, G.J. *The Nature of Time* (Penguin, Harmondsworth, Middlesex) 1975.

Wiles, Maurice *Working Papers in Doctrine* (SCM, London) 1976.

Wiles, Maurice and Santer, Mark, eds. *Documents in Early Christian Thought* (Cambridge University Press, Cambridge and New York) 1975.

Wilson, Edgar *The Mental as Physical* (Routledge, London and Boston) 1979.

Wolfsen, H.A. *The Philosophy of the Church Fathers*, 3rd ed. (Harvard University Press, Cambridge, Mass.) 1970.

Zaehner, R.C. *Mysticism Sacred and Profane* (Oxford University Press, Oxford and New York) 1957.

Index